RESUMES
FOR
FIRST-TIME
JOB HUNTERS

Professional Resumes Series

RESUMES FOR FIRST-TIME JOB HUNTERS

The Editors of
VGM Career Books

Second Edition

VGM Career Books
NTC/Contemporary Publishing Group

Library of Congress Cataloging-in-Publication Data

Resumes for first-time job hunters / Marjorie Eberts, [editor]. — 2nd ed.
   p.   cm. — (VGM professional resumes series)
   ISBN 0-658-00454-9
   1. Resumes (Employment)   I. Eberts, Marjorie.   II. Series.
HF5383.R455 2000
808'.06665—dc21   00-39268
                                                                CIP

The editors gratefully acknowledge Marjorie Eberts for her help
in the writing and production of this book.

Interior design by City Desktop Productions

Published by VGM Career Books
A division of NTC/Contemporary Publishing Group, Inc.
4255 West Touhy Avenue, Lincolnwood (Chicago), Illinois 60712-1975 U.S.A.
Copyright © 2000 by NTC/Contemporary Publishing Group, Inc.
Printed in the United States of America
International Standard Book Number: 0-658-00454-9

2 3 4 5 6 7 8 9 0 VLP VLP 0 5 4 3 2 1

RESUMES
FOR
FIRST-TIME
JOB HUNTERS

Contents

Introduction

Your resume is your first impression on a prospective employer. Though you may be articulate, intelligent, and charming in person, a poor resume may prevent you from ever having the opportunity to demonstrate your interpersonal skills, because a poor resume may prevent you from ever being called for an interview. While few people have ever been hired solely on the basis of their resume, a well-written, well-organized resume can go a long way toward helping you land an interview. Your resume's main purpose is to get you that interview. The rest is up to you and the employer. If you both feel that you are right for the job and the job is right for you, chances are you will be hired.

A resume must catch the reader's attention yet still be easy to read and to the point. Resume styles have changed over the years. Today, brief and focused resumes are preferred. No longer do employers have the patience, or the time, to review several pages of solid type. A resume should be only one page long, if possible. Time is a precious commodity in today's business world and the resume that is concise and straightforward will usually be the one that gets noticed.

Let's not make the mistake, though, of assuming that writing a brief resume means that you can take less care in preparing it. A successful resume takes time and thought, and if you are willing to make the effort, the rewards are well worth it. Think of your resume as a sales tool with the product being you. You want to sell yourself to a prospective employer. This book is designed to help you prepare a resume that will further your career—to land that next job, or first job, or to return to the workforce after years of absence. So, read on. Make the effort and reap the rewards that a strong resume can bring to your career. Let's get to it!

The Elements of a Good Resume

A winning resume is made of the elements that employers are most interested in seeing when reviewing a job applicant. These basic elements are the essential ingredients of a successful resume and become the actual sections of your resume. The following is a list of elements that may be used in a resume. Some are essential, some are optional. We will be discussing these in this chapter to give you a better understanding of each element's role in the makeup of your resume:

1. Heading

2. Objective

3. Work Experience

4. Education

5. Honors

6. Activities

7. Certificates and Licenses

8. Professional Memberships

9. Special Skills

10. Personal Information

11. References

The first step in preparing your resume is to gather information about yourself and your past accomplishments. Later you will refine this information, rewrite it in the most effective language, and organize it into the most attractive layout. First, let's take a look at each of these important elements individually.

Heading

The heading may seem to be a simple enough element in your resume, but be careful not to take it lightly. The heading should be placed at the top of your resume and should include your name, home address, and telephone numbers. If you can take calls at your current place of business, include your business number, since most employers will attempt to contact you during the business day. If this is not possible, or if you can afford it, purchase an answering machine that allows you to retrieve your messages while you are away from home. This way you can make sure you don't miss important phone calls. Always include your phone number on your resume. It is crucial that when prospective employers need to have immediate contact with you, they can.

Objective

When seeking a particular career path, it is important to list a job objective on your resume. This statement helps employers know the direction that you see yourself heading, so that they can determine whether your goals are in line with the position available. The objective is normally one sentence long and describes your employment goals clearly and concisely. See the sample resumes in this book for examples of objective statements.

The job objective will vary depending on the type of person you are, the field you are in, and the type of goals you have. It can be either specific or general, but it should always be to the point.

In some cases, this element is not necessary, but usually it is a good idea to include your objective. It gives your possible future employer an idea of where you are coming from and where you want to go.

The objective statement is better left out, however, if you are uncertain of the exact title of the job you seek. In such a case, the inclusion of an overly specific objective statement could result in your not being considered for a variety of acceptable positions; be sure to incorporate this information in your cover letter instead.

Work Experience

This element is arguably the most important of them all. It will provide the central focus of your resume, so it is necessary that this section be as complete as possible. Only by examining your work experience in depth can you get to the heart of your accomplishments and present them in a way that demonstrates the strength of your qualifications. Of course, someone just out of school will have less work experience than someone who has been working for a number of years, but the amount of information isn't the most important thing—rather, how it is presented, and how it highlights you as a person and as a worker will be what counts.

As you work on this section of your resume, be aware of the need for accuracy. You'll want to include all necessary information about each of your jobs, including job title, dates, employer, city, state, responsibilities, special projects, and accomplishments. Be sure to only list company accomplishments for which you were directly responsible. If you haven't participated in any special projects, that's all right—this area may not be relevant to certain jobs.

The most common way to list your work experience is in *reverse chronological order*. In other words, start with your most recent job and work your way backward. This way your prospective employer sees your current (and often most important) job before seeing your past jobs. Your most recent position, if the most important, should also be the one that includes the most information, as compared to your previous positions. If you are just out of school, show your summer employment and part-time work, though in this case your education will most likely be more important than your work experience.

The following worksheets will help you gather information about your past jobs.

WORK EXPERIENCE

Job One:

Job Title _____

Dates _____

Employer _____

City, State _____

Major Duties _____

_____

_____

_____

_____

_____

_____

_____

Special Projects _____

_____

_____

_____

Accomplishments _____

_____

_____

_____

_____

_____

_____

_____

Job Two:

Job Title _____

Dates _____

Employer _____

City, State _____

Major Duties _____

_____

_____

_____

_____

_____

_____

_____

Special Projects _____

_____

_____

_____

Accomplishments _____

_____

_____

_____

_____

_____

_____

_____

Job Three:

Job Title _____

Dates _____

Employer _____

City, State _____

Major Duties _____

_____

_____

_____

_____

_____

_____

_____

Special Projects _____

_____

_____

_____

Accomplishments _____

_____

_____

_____

_____

_____

_____

_____

Job Four:

Job Title _____

Dates _____

Employer _____

City, State _____

Major Duties _____

_____

_____

_____

_____

_____

_____

_____

Special Projects _____

_____

_____

_____

Accomplishments _____

_____

_____

_____

_____

_____

_____

_____

Education

Education is the second most important element of a resume. Your educational background is often a deciding factor in an employer's decision to hire you. Be sure to stress your accomplishments in school with the same finesse that you stressed your accomplishments at work. If you are looking for your first job, your education will be your greatest asset, since your work experience will most likely be minimal. In this case, the education section becomes the most important. You will want to be sure to include any degrees or certificates you received, your major area of concentration, any honors, and any relevant activities. Again, be sure to list your most recent schooling first. If you have completed graduate-level work, begin with that and work in reverse chronological order through your undergraduate education. If you have completed an undergraduate degree, you may choose whether to list your high school experience or not. This should be done only if your high school grade point average was well above average.

The following worksheets will help you gather information for this section of your resume. Also included are supplemental worksheets for honors and for activities. Sometimes honors and activities are listed in a section separate from education, most often near the end of the resume.

EDUCATION

School One _____

Major or Area of Concentration _____

Degree _____

Dates _____

School Two _____

Major or Area of Concentration _____

Degree _____

Dates _____

Honors

Here you should list any awards, honors, or memberships in honorary societies that you have received. Usually these are of an academic nature, but they can also be for special achievement in sports, clubs, or other school activities. Always be sure to include the name of the organization honoring you and the date(s) received. Use the worksheet below to help gather your honors information.

HONORS

Honor One _____

Awarding Organization _____

Date(s) _____

Honor Two _____

Awarding Organization _____

Date(s) _____

Honor Three _____

Awarding Organization _____

Date(s) _____

Honor Four _____

Awarding Organization _____

Date(s) _____

Activities

You may have been active in different organizations or clubs during your years at school; often an employer will look at such involvement as evidence of initiative and dedication. Your ability to take an active role, and even a leadership role, in a group should be included on your resume. Use the worksheet provided to list your activities and accomplishments in this area. In general, you should exclude any organization whose name indicates the race, creed, sex, age, marital status, color, or nation of origin of its members.

ACTIVITIES

Organization/Activity _____

Accomplishments _____

_____

_____

Organization/Activity _____

Accomplishments _____

_____

_____

Organization/Activity _____

Accomplishments _____

_____

_____

Organization/Activity _____

Accomplishments _____

_____

_____

As your work experience increases through the years, your school activities and honors will play less of a role in your resume, and eventually you will most likely only list your degree and any major honors you received. This is due to the fact that, as time goes by, your job performance becomes the most important element in your resume. Through time, your resume should change to reflect this.

Certificates and Licenses

The next potential element of your resume is certificates and licenses. You should list these if the job you are seeking requires them and you, of course, have acquired them. If you have applied for a license, but have not yet received it, use the phrase "application pending."

License requirements vary by state. If you have moved or are planning to move to another state, be sure to check with that state's board or licensing agency for all licensing requirements.

Always be sure that all of the information you list is completely accurate. Locate copies of your licenses and certificates and check the exact date and name of the accrediting agency. Use the following worksheet to list your licenses and certificates.

CERTIFICATES AND LICENSES

Name of License _____

Licensing Agency _____

Date Issued _____

Name of License _____

Licensing Agency _____

Date Issued _____

Name of License _____

Licensing Agency _____

Date Issued _____

Professional Memberships

Another potential element in your resume is a section listing professional memberships. Use this section to list involvement in professional associations, unions, and similar organizations. It is to your advantage to list any professional memberships that pertain to the job you are seeking. Be sure to include the dates of your involvement and whether you took part in any special activities or held any offices within the organization. Use the following worksheet to gather your information.

PROFESSIONAL MEMBERSHIPS

Name of Organization _____

Offices Held _____

Activities _____

Dates _____

Name of Organization _____

Offices Held _____

Activities _____

Dates _____

Name of Organization _____

Offices Held _____

Activities _____

Dates _____

Name of Organization _____

Offices Held _____

Activities _____

Dates _____

Special Skills

This section of your resume is for mentioning any special abilities you have that could relate to the job you are seeking. This is the part of your resume where you have the opportunity to demonstrate certain talents and experiences that are not necessarily a part of your educational or work experience. Common examples include fluency in a foreign language or knowledge of a particular computer application.

Special skills can encompass a wide range of your talents—remember that whatever skills you list should relate to the type of work you are looking for.

Personal Information

Some people include "Personal" information on their resumes. This is not generally recommended, but you might wish to include it if you think that something in your personal life, such as a hobby or talent, has some bearing on the position you are seeking. This type of information is often referred to at the beginning of an interview, when it is used as an "ice breaker." Of course, personal information regarding age, marital status, race, religion, or sexual preference should never appear on any resume.

References

References are not usually listed on the resume, but a prospective employer needs to know that you have references who may be contacted if necessary. All that is necessary to include in your resume regarding references is a sentence at the bottom stating, "References are available upon request." If a prospective employer requests a list of references, be sure to have one ready. Also, check with whomever you list to see if it is all right for you to use them as a reference. Forewarn them that they may receive a call regarding a reference for you. This way they can be prepared to give you the best reference possible.

Chapter 2

Writing Your Resume

Now that you have gathered all of the information for each of the sections of your resume, it's time to write out each section in a way that will get the attention of whoever is reviewing it. The type of language you use in your resume will affect its success. You want to take the information you have gathered and translate it into a language that will cause a potential employer to sit up and take notice.

Resume writing is not like expository writing or creative writing. It embodies a functional, direct writing style and focuses on the use of action words. By using action words in your writing, you more effectively stress past accomplishments. Action words demonstrate your initiative and highlight your talents. Always use verbs that show strength and reflect the qualities of a "doer." By using action words, you characterize yourself as a person who takes action, and this will impress potential employers.

The following is a list of verbs commonly used in resume writing. Use this list to choose the action words that can help your resume become a strong one:

administered	billed
advised	built
analyzed	carried out
arranged	channeled
assembled	collected
assumed responsibility	communicated

compiled	maintained
completed	managed
conducted	met with
contacted	motivated
contracted	negotiated
coordinated	operated
counseled	orchestrated
created	ordered
cut	organized
designed	oversaw
determined	performed
developed	planned
directed	prepared
dispatched	presented
distributed	produced
documented	programmed
edited	published
established	purchased
expanded	recommended
functioned as	recorded
gathered	reduced
handled	referred
hired	represented
implemented	researched
improved	reviewed
inspected	saved
interviewed	screened
introduced	served as
invented	served on

sold	tested
suggested	trained
supervised	typed
taught	wrote

Now take a look at the information you put down on the work experience worksheets. Take that information and rewrite it in paragraph form, using verbs to highlight your actions and accomplishments. Let's look at an example, remembering that what matters here is the writing style, and not the particular job responsibilities given in our sample.

WORK EXPERIENCE
Regional Sales Manager

Manager of sales representatives from seven states. Responsible for 12 food chain accounts in the East. In charge of directing the sales force in planned selling toward specific goals. Supervisor and trainer of new sales representatives. Consulting for customers in the areas of inventory management and quality control.

Special Projects: Coordinator and sponsor of annual food industry sales seminar.

Accomplishments: Monthly regional volume went up 25 percent during my tenure while, at the same time, a proper sales/cost ratio was maintained. Customer/company relations improved significantly.

Below is the rewritten version of this information, using action words. Notice how much stronger it sounds.

WORK EXPERIENCE
Regional Sales Manager

Managed sales representatives from seven states. Handled 12 food chain accounts in the eastern United States. Directed the sales force in planned selling toward specific goals. Supervised and trained new sales representatives. Consulted for customers in the areas of inventory management and quality control. Coordinated and sponsored the annual Food Industry Seminar. Increased monthly regional volume 25 percent and helped to improve customer/company relations during my tenure.

Another way of constructing the work experience section is by using actual job descriptions. Job descriptions are rarely written using the proper resume language, but they do include all the information necessary to create this section of your resume. Take the description of one of the jobs you are including on your resume (if you have access to it), and turn it into an action-oriented paragraph. Below is an example of a job description followed by a version of the same description written using action words. Again, pay attention to the style of writing, as the details of your own work experience will be unique.

WORK EXPERIENCE
Public Administrator I

Responsibilities: Coordinate and direct public services to meet the needs of the nation, state, or community. Analyze problems; work with special committees and public agencies; recommend solutions to governing bodies.

Aptitudes and Skills: Ability to relate to and communicate with people; solve complex problems through analysis; plan, organize, and implement policies and programs. Knowledge of political systems; financial management; personnel administration; program evaluation; organizational theory.

WORK EXPERIENCE
Public Administrator I

Wrote pamphlets and conducted discussion groups to inform citizens of legislative processes and consumer issues. Organized and supervised 25 interviewers. Trained interviewers in effective communication skills.

Now that you have learned how to word your resume, you are ready for the next step in your quest for a winning resume: assembly and layout.

Chapter 3

Assembly and Layout

A t this point, you've gathered all the necessary information for your resume, and you've rewritten it using the language necessary to impress potential employers. Your next step is to assemble these elements in a logical order and lay them out on the page neatly and attractively to achieve the desired effect: getting that interview.

Assembly

The order of the elements in a resume makes a difference in its overall effect. Obviously, you would not want to put your name and address in the middle of the resume or your special skills section at the top. You want to put the elements in an order that stresses your most important achievements, not the less pertinent information. For example, if you recently graduated from school and have no full-time work experience, you will want to list your education before you list any part-time jobs you may have held during school. On the other hand, if you have been gainfully employed for several years and currently hold an important position in your company, you will want to list your work experience ahead of your education, which has become less pertinent with time.

There are some elements that are always included in your resume and some that are optional. Following is a list of essential and optional elements:

Essential	Optional
Name	Job Objective
Address	Honors
Phone Number	Special Skills
Work Experience	Professional Memberships
Education	Activities
References Phrase	Certificates and Licenses
	Personal Information

Your choice of optional sections depends on your own background and employment needs. Always use information that puts you and your abilities in a favorable light. If your honors are impressive, then be sure to include them in your resume. If your activities in school demonstrate particular talents necessary for the job you are seeking, then allow space for a section on activities. Each resume is unique, just as each person is unique.

Types of Resumes

So far, our discussion about resumes has involved the most common type—the *reverse chronological* resume, in which your most recent job is listed first and so on. This is the type of resume usually preferred by human resources directors, and it is the one most frequently used. However, in some cases this style of presentation is not the most effective way to highlight your skills and accomplishments.

For someone reentering the workforce after many years or someone looking to change career fields, the *functional resume* may work best. This type of resume focuses more on achievement and less on the sequence of your work history. In the functional resume, your experience is presented by what you have accomplished and the skills you have developed in your past work.

A functional resume can be assembled from the same information you collected for your chronological resume. The main difference lies in how you organize this information. Essentially, the work experience section becomes two sections, with your job duties and accomplishments comprising one section and your employer's name, city, state, your position, and the dates employed making up another section. The first section is placed near the top of the resume, just below the job objective section, and can be called *Accomplishments* or *Achievements*. The second section, containing the bare essentials of your employment history, should come after the accomplishments section and can be titled *Work Experience* or *Employment History*. The other sections of your resume remain the same. The work experience section is the only one affected in the functional resume. By placing the section that focuses on your achievements first, you draw attention to these achievements. This puts less emphasis on who you worked for and more emphasis on what you did and what you are capable of doing.

For someone changing careers, emphasis on skills and achievements is essential. The identities of previous employers, which may be unrelated to one's new job field, need to be downplayed. The functional resume accomplishes this task. For someone reentering the workforce after many years, a functional resume is the obvious choice. If you lack full-time work experience, you will need to draw attention away from this fact and instead focus on your skills and abilities gained possibly through volunteer activities or part-time work. Education may also play a more important role in this resume.

Which type of resume is right for you depends on your own personal circumstances. It may be helpful to create a chronological and a functional resume and then compare the two to find out which is more suitable. The sample resumes found in this book include both chronological and functional resumes. Use these resumes as guides to help you decide on the content and appearance of your own resume.

Layout

Once you have decided which elements to include in your resume and you have arranged them in an order that makes sense and emphasizes your achievements and abilities, then it is time to work on the physical layout of your resume.

There is no single appropriate layout that applies to every resume, but there are a few basic rules to follow in putting your resume on paper:

1. Leave a comfortable margin on the sides, top, and bottom of the page (usually 1 to 1½ inches).

2. Use appropriate spacing between the sections (usually 2 to 3 line spaces are adequate).

3. Be consistent in the *type* of headings you use for the different sections of your resume. For example, if you capitalize the heading EMPLOYMENT HISTORY, don't use initial capitals and underlining for a heading of equal importance, such as Education.

CHRONOLOGICAL RESUME

DAVID P. JENKINS

3663 N. Coldwater Canyon • North Hollywood, CA 90390
818/555-3472• 818/555-3678

JOB OBJECTIVE

A position as a sales/marketing manager where I can use my knowledge and experience by combining high-volume selling of major accounts with an administrative ability that increases sales through encouragement of sales team.

EMPLOYMENT HISTORY

Tribor Industries, Los Angeles, CA
Regional Sales Manager, 1993 - present

Managed sales of all product lines in western markets for a leading maker of linens. Represented five corporate divisions of the company with sales in excess of $3,000,000 annually. Directed and motivated a sales force of 12 sales representatives in planned selling to achieve company goals.

Tribor Industries, Los Angeles, CA
District Manager, 1988 - 1993

Acted as sales representative for the Los Angeles metropolitan area. Built both wholesale and dealer distribution substantially during my tenure. Promoted to Regional Manager after five years of service.

American Office Supply, Chicago, IL
Assistant Sales Manager, 1984 - 1988

Handled both internal and external sales and marketing, including samples, advertising, and pricing. Served as company sales representative and sold a variety of office supplies to retail stores.

EDUCATION

University of Michigan, Ann Arbor, MI
B.A. Business Administration, 1983
Major Field: Management

SEMINARS

National Management Association Seminar, 1992
Purdue University Seminars, 1995, 1997

PROFESSIONAL MEMBERSHIPS

Sales and Marketing Association of Los Angeles
National Association of Market Developers

REFERENCES

Available upon request

FUNCTIONAL RESUME

Sara Woods
4400 Sunset Blvd., Los Angeles, CA 90028
(213) 555-8989 • (213) 555-4950

Objective

A position in sales management.

Achievements

- Planned successful strategies to identify and develop new accounts.
- Increased sales by at least 20 percent each year as District Sales Manager.
- Researched and analyzed market conditions in order to seek out new customers.
- Developed weekly and monthly sales strategies.
- Supervised seven sales representatives.
- Conducted field visits to solve customer complaints.
- Maintained daily customer contact to ensure good customer/company relations.
- Wrote product information fliers and distributed them through a direct-mail program.

Work Experience

Southern California Fruit Co.
Los Angeles, CA
District Sales Manager, 1994 - present

L.A. Freight Co.
Los Angeles, CA
Account Executive, 1992 - 1994

Handlemen & Associates
Santa Rita, CA
Sales Representative, 1991 - 1992

Education

University of Colorado, Boulder, CO
B.A., June 1991
Major: Management
Minor: Political Science
GPA: 3.3/4.0

Professional Memberships

- Southern California Sales Association, Treasurer, 1996 - 1998
- Los Angeles Chamber of Commerce, 1994 - present

Special Skills

- Experienced with Lotus and WordPerfect.

References

Provided on request.

4. Always try to fit your resume onto one page. If you are having trouble fitting all your information onto one page, perhaps you are trying to say too much. Edit out any repetitive or unnecessary information or shorten descriptions of earlier jobs. Be ruthless. Maybe you've included too many optional sections.

Don't let the idea of having to tell every detail about your life get in the way of producing a resume that is simple and straightforward. The more compact your resume, the easier it is to read and the better an impression it will make for you.

In some cases, the resume will not fit on a single page, even after extensive editing. In such cases, the resume should be printed on two pages so as not to compromise clarity or appearance. Each page of a two-page resume should be marked clearly with your name and the page number, for example, "Judith Ramirez, page 1 of 2." The pages should be stapled together.

Experiment with various layouts until you find one that looks good to you. Always show your final layout to other people and ask them what they like or dislike about it, and what impresses them most about your resume. Make sure that is what you want most to emphasize. If it isn't, you may want to consider making changes in your layout until the necessary information is emphasized. Use the sample resumes in this book to get some ideas for laying out your resume.

Putting Your Resume in Print

Your resume should be typed or printed on good quality 8½″ × 11″ bond paper. You want to make as good an impression as possible with your resume; therefore, quality paper is a necessity. If you have access to a word processor with a good printer, or know of someone who does, make use of it. Typewritten resumes should only be used when there are no other options available.

After you have produced a clean original, make duplicate copies of it. Usually a copy shop is your best bet for producing copies without smudges or streaks. Make sure you have the copy shop use quality bond paper for all copies of your resume. Ask for a sample copy before they run your entire order. After copies are made, check each copy for cleanliness and clarity.

Another more costly option is to have your resume typeset and printed by a printer. This provides the most attractive resume of all. If you anticipate needing a lot of copies of your resume, the cost of having it typeset may be justified.

Proofreading

After you have finished typing the master copy of your resume and before you have it copied or printed, thoroughly check it for typing and spelling errors. Have several people read it over just in case you have missed an error. Misspelled words and typing mistakes do not make a good impression on a prospective employer, as they are a bad reflection on your writing ability and your attention to detail. With thorough and conscientious proofreading, these mistakes can be avoided.

The following are some rules of capitalization and punctuation that may come in handy when proofreading your resume:

RULES OF CAPITALIZATION

- Capitalize proper nouns, such as names of schools, colleges, and universities; names of companies; and brand names of products.
- Capitalize major words in the names and titles of books, tests, and articles that appear in the body of your resume.
- Capitalize words in major section headings of your resume.
- Do not capitalize words just because they seem important.
- When in doubt, consult a manual of style such as *Words into Type* (Prentice Hall), or *The Chicago Manual of Style* (The University of Chicago Press). Your local library can help you locate these and other reference books.

RULES OF PUNCTUATION

- Use a comma to separate words in a series.
- Use a semicolon to separate series of words that already include commas within the series.
- Use a semicolon to separate independent clauses that are not joined by a conjunction.

- Use a period to end a sentence.

- Use a colon to show that examples or details follow that will expand or amplify the preceding phrase.

- Avoid the use of dashes.

- Avoid the use of brackets.

- If you use any punctuation in an unusual way in your resume, be consistent in its use.

- Whenever you are uncertain, consult a style manual.

Chapter 4

The Cover Letter

Once your resume has been assembled, laid out, and printed to your satisfaction, the next step before distribution is to write your cover letter. Though there may be instances when you deliver your resume in person, you usually send it through the mail. Resumes sent through the mail always need an accompanying letter that briefly introduces you and your resume. The purpose of the cover letter is to get a potential employer to read your resume, just as the purpose of your resume is to get that same potential employer to call you for an interview.

Like your resume, your cover letter should be clean, neat, and direct. A cover letter usually includes the following information:

1. Your name and address (unless it already appears on your personal letterhead).

2. The date.

3. The name and address of the person and company to whom you are sending your resume.

4. The salutation ("Dear Mr." or "Dear Ms." followed by the person's last name, or "To Whom It May Concern" if you are answering a blind ad).

5. An opening paragraph explaining why you are writing (in response to an ad, the result of a previous meeting, at the suggestion of someone you both know) and indicating that you are interested in whatever job is being offered.

6. One or two more paragraphs that tell why you want to work for the company and what qualifications and experience you can bring to that company.

7. A final paragraph that closes the letter and requests that you be contacted for an interview.

8. The closing ("Sincerely," or "Yours truly," followed by your signature with your name typed under it).

Your cover letter, including all of the information above, should be no more than one page in length. The language used should be polite, businesslike, and to the point. Do not attempt to tell your life story in the cover letter. A long and cluttered letter will only serve to put off the reader. Remember, you only need to mention a few of your accomplishments and skills in the cover letter. The rest of your information is in your resume. Every achievement should not be mentioned twice. If your cover letter is a success, your resume will be read and all pertinent information reviewed by your prospective employer.

Producing the Cover Letter

Cover letters should always be individualized, since they are always written to particular individuals and companies. Never use a form letter for your cover letter. Cover letters cannot be copied or reproduced like resumes. Each one should be as personal as possible. Of course, once you have written and rewritten your first cover letter to the point where you are satisfied with it, you can use similar wording in subsequent letters.

After you have typed your cover letter on quality bond paper, proofread it as thoroughly as you did your resume. Again, spelling errors are a sure sign of carelessness, and you don't want that to be a part of your first impression on a prospective employer. Handle the letter and resume carefully to avoid any smudges, and then mail both your cover letter and resume in an appropriately sized envelope. Keep an accurate record of all the resumes you send out and the results of each mailing, either in a separate notebook or on individual index cards.

Numerous sample cover letters appear at the end of this book. Use them as models for your own cover letter or to get an idea of how cover letters are put together. Remember, every cover letter is unique and depends on the particular circumstances of the individual writing it and the job for which he or she is applying.

Now the job of writing your resume and cover letter is complete. About a week after mailing resumes and cover letters to potential employers, contact them by telephone. Confirm that your resume arrived, and ask whether an interview might be possible. Getting your foot in the door during this call is half the battle of a job search, and a strong resume and cover letter will help you immeasurably.

Chapter 5

Sample Resumes

This chapter contains dozens of sample resumes for people pursuing a wide variety of jobs and careers.

There are many different styles of resumes in terms of graphic layout and presentation of information. These samples also represent people with varying amounts of education and work experience. Use these samples to model your own resume after. Choose one resume, or borrow elements from several different resumes to help you construct your own.

Timothy J. Comer

3825 West Thunderbird Way • Three Lakes, WI 54562 • (715) 555-1878

Objective: Summer employment in which I can work and serve people. Salaried position preferred.

Education: Three Lakes High School, 1996 - 2000
                General education/Honors and Advanced Placement courses

Experience:

1997 - 1999   **Snowy Sam's Restaurant**, Eagle River, WI; Sales and Cleaning. Responsibilities included opening, preparing all food, dealing with customers, keeping track of money, balancing the money at the end of the day, and securing the building.

Capabilities: • Excellent organizational skills
                • Responsible
                • Proficient in the use of cash registers and Macintosh computers
                • Able to work with people
                • Skilled in working independently

Achievements:

1999 - 2000   • Commissioner of Homecoming and Elections, Associated Student Body; Principal's Highest Honor Roll

1998 - 1999   • Class Treasurer; Principal's Honor Roll

1997 - 1998   • Commissioner of Desegregation, Associated Student Body; Principal's Honor Roll

1996 - 1997   • House of Representatives Alternate, Principal's Honor Roll

Affiliations: • Three Lakes Football Team
                Three Lakes Track-and-Field Team

Awards: • Outstanding Leadership Award, Class of 2000

                • Three Lakes Football Scout Team Player of the Year, 1999

References: Available upon request.

MICHAEL SUTHERLAND
2757 Dolphin Dr. • Arnold, MD 21012 • (301) 555-5390

Education   **UCLA School of Theater, Film, and TV**, Fall 1999
- Comprehensive Major: Directing and Theater Management

Arnold High School, June 1999
- Forensics Competitive Speech Team (4 years)
- Drama and Musical Productions (3 years)

Awards
- Bank of Maryland Fine Arts Award -
  2nd place Region Finals Scholarship, 1999
- Veterans of Foreign Wars Speech Award, 1998 and 1999
- Student of the Year - Arnold High School, 1998
- Boys' State Delegate, 1998
- 21st place in State Forensics for Thematic Interpretation
  (Pieces included: *Torch Song Trilogy*, *Into the Woods*,
  Brighton Beach Memoirs, *Measure for Measure*), 1998
- Rotary Speech Award, 1996 and 1997
- Walter Johnson Musical Comedy Award
  at Anne Arundel Community Stage, 1996

Performance Theater Experience

- Director, Collaborator, and Performer, *AIDS Teen Theater*, 1999
- "Billy Crocker" in *Anything Goes*, 1998
- "Vincentio" in *Taming of the Shrew*, 1998
- "Albert" in *Bye-Bye Birdie*, 1997
- "Frank Butler" in *Annie Get Your Gun*, 1996
- "Charlie" in *Charlie and the Chocolate Factory*, 1996
- "Ed" in *You Can't Take It with You*, 1996
- Writer and Performer, *AIDS Teen Theater*, 1995 and 1996

Technical and Managing Theater Experience

Anne Arundel Community Stage
- Production Assistant - *Fiddler on the Roof*, 1999
- Assistant Stage Manager - *Into the Woods*, 1997
- Assistant Stage Manager - *Camelot*, 1996
- Chorus and Stagehand - *Evita*, 1995
- Stagehand - *My Fair Lady*, 1995

Peace Child
- Assistant Stage Manager, Props Assistant, 1997
- Assistant Technical Director USA/USSR Production, 1996

References   Available upon request

Jennifer Rosales
381 Ponderosa Avenue
Albuquerque, NM 87198
(505) 555-3578

Work Experience

August 18, 1999, to May 22, 2000
Food Service Worker. Kentucky Fried Chicken, Albuquerque, NM.
Responsibilities: Taking and preparing food orders, running cash register,
stocking supplies, and cleaning kitchen and eating areas.

May 10, 1999, to August 1, 1999
Receptionist. Santa Fe Real Estate Company, Albuquerque, NM.
Responsibilities: Answering phones and calling customers for
further information pertaining to their homes.

Prior to May 1999
Babysitter

Other Experience

- I am a student in O.W.E., "Outside Work Experience,"
  learning about jobs and future careers.
- I am fluent in Spanish.
- I was a camp counselor working with children aged 11 - 13,
  assisting with sports and recreational activities.
- I was a member of the following Albuquerque High School groups:
  Unity Among Us, Students in Christian Fellowship, F.N.L., Student Body Council,
  and Going Places Academically.
- I am involved with church activities.

Education

- I am a graduate of Albuquerque High School, 2000.
- My grade point average was 2.85/4.00.
- My future educational plans are to attend National College.

References

Available upon request.

JONATHAN DEAN COURIER
8638 Walter Drive • Evanston, IL 60204 • (708) 555-4825

CAREER OBJECTIVE
An engineering position involving civil/structural analysis and design.

EDUCATION

Northwestern University
Master of Science degree in Civil Engineering
Credits completed toward degree: 21/33

Bachelor of Science degree in Civil Engineering, 1998
Major: Structural Engineering
Minors: Geotechnical Engineering and Construction

Engineer in Training, Illinois

WORK EXPERIENCE

Summer 1999   **Elijah's Architects & Engineers, Inc., Chicago, IL**
Engineering Intern
Worked in the structural division, dealing with the design of
criminal justice and educational facilities.

1998 - 1999   **School of Civil Engineering, Northwestern University**
Teaching Assistant
Helped with Architectural Engineering, Structural Steel Design,
and Senior Design classes; tasks included instruction and grading
of students.

Summer 1998   **Civil Engineering Buildings, Northwestern University**
Building Receiving Technician
Handled various assignments during the final construction phases
of new additions.

ACTIVITIES AND HONORS
Distinguished Student, Fall 1997
Student Member, American Society of Civil Engineers
Theta Chi Honorary: Marshal, Spring 1997, and President, Fall 1997

REFERENCES AVAILABLE UPON REQUEST

MIGUEL ROSAS

Campus Address
434 J. Pierce Hall
Arizona State University
Tempe, AZ 85287
(602) 555-1328

Permanent Address
836 High Street
Reno, NV 89512
(702) 555-7206

OBJECTIVE:
To obtain a position as an engineer in the field of civil engineering.

EDUCATION:
Arizona State University - 1999
B.S. Civil Engineering with a structural engineering emphasis.

EXPERIENCE:
PRIORITY COURIER, Reno, NV.
Courier
• Picked up and delivered bank bags.
• Handled special delivery of packages and letters for customers.
Summer 1998

YOUTH CONSERVATION CORPS, Reno, NV.
Maintenance Worker
• Involved with upkeep and improvement of state park trails.
• Constructed fence to protect state park nature preserve.
Summer 1997

CHARLIE'S BAR AND GRILL, Reno, NV.
Busboy
• Cleared tables.
• Replenished supplies as needed.
Summers 1992 through 1996

ACTIVITIES:
Eagle Scout, Boy Scouts of America.
Member, National Eagle Scout Association.
Member, American Society of Civil Engineers.

PERSONAL:
• Proficient with CAD.
• Willing to relocate.

REFERENCES:
Available upon request.

JOSEPHINE ELIZABETH CROCKER
P.O. Box 317A
Trenton, NJ 08625
(609) 555-4832

OBJECTIVE: To gain an entry-level position in the environmental field with a firm offering advanced training.

EDUCATION AND TRAINING

- B.S. Environmental Health Science, Trenton State College, Trenton, NJ
  1996 - 2000. 3.2 GPA in major, 2.8 GPA overall.

COURSES

Principles and Practices of Environmental Health
Accident and Disaster Control
Technical Seminar in Environmental Health
Public Health Administration
Microbiology
Epidemiology
Health Biostatistics
Public Health Education
Administrative Seminar
Practicum in Environmental Health
Organic Chemistry
Applied Microbiology

- Internship, Oneida County Health Department, Environmental Division.
  May - August 1998.
- Internship, Vilas County Health Department, Environmental Division.
  May - August 1997.

AWARDS AND HONORS

- Inter-sorority Council Outstanding Greek Woman, 1999.
- Who's Who Among Students in American Universities and Colleges, 1999.
- Order of Chi Omega Greek Honorary, 1998.
- Inter-sorority Council Most Outstanding Spring President, 1998.
- Inter-sorority Council Most Outstanding Chapter Member, 1997.
- Society of Distinguished Collegiate Americans, 1997.

ACTIVITIES

- Chi Omega, President.
- Inter-sorority Council, Chief Justice of Judicial Board.
- UCP Telethon, Phone Bank Coordinator.

REFERENCES: Will be provided on request.

CINDY MILLER   6652 E. Laurel Rd. • Newark, OH 43055 • (614) 555-4331

CAREER OBJECTIVE
To secure a position emphasizing engineering and managerial skills with a firm engaged in building construction operations.

EDUCATION
Rutgers - The State University of New Jersey:
College of Engineering, New Brunswick, NJ
> *Bachelor of Science, May 1999   GPA: 3.5/4.0*
> *Major: Construction Engineering and Management*

Significant Courses
- Construction Estimating
- Construction Scheduling
- Computer Programming
- Construction Management
- Labor Relations
- Finance and Accounting
- Technical Graphics
- Surveying

Curriculum focused on group projects: Developed complete schematic design and preliminary construction plans for a real facility.

EMPLOYMENT EXPERIENCE
Granite Construction Company, Watsonville, CA
Field Engineer/Scheduler   Summer 1998   60 hours/week
Responsibilities:
- project layout
- project checkout
- scheduling of job activities
- organizational preparation

Granite Construction Company, Birmingham, AL
Estimator   Summer 1997   48 hours/week
Responsibilities:
- document distribution
- quantity takeoffs from prints
- data entry
- conceptual takeoffs from sketches

Granite Construction Company, Fort Worth, TX
Field Engineer/Tracker   Summer 1996   40 hours/week
Responsibilities:
- project layout
- project checkout
- tracking job progression
- laborer

ACTIVITIES
- Associated Builders and Contractors: advertising committee
- Intramural team sports: volleyball and badminton

REFERENCES AVAILABLE UPON REQUEST

SHARI T. LUISO

Permanent: Current:

256 Dove Lane   P.O. Box 1259

Tampa, FL 33614   Evanston, IL 60204

(813) 555-6901   (847) 555-3246

EDUCATION:

Northwestern University, Evanston, IL.

Bachelor of Arts degree in Public Policy Studies, May 1999.

Course work: Macroeconomics, Microeconomics, Economic Analysis for Public Policy Making, Leadership and Policy Change, Policy Analysis for Public Policy Making, Managerial Effectiveness, Policy Choice and Value Conflict, Analytical Methods for Public Policy Making, Statistical Quantitative Political Analysis.

Sorbonne, Paris, France.

Course work: French language, art, and history.

Sorbonne College Faculty Honors List, Fall 1998.

WORK EXPERIENCE:

Council for Entrepreneurial Development, Durham, NC.

Management Intern. Oversee weekly "Entrepreneur's Page" in *Triangle Business Journal*: contact area business leaders to match article topics with knowledgeable authors, personally write additional pieces, edit and compile all contributions.

June 1998 - present.

Triangle Business Journal, Raleigh, NC.

Advertising and Promotion Intern. Created advertisements, researched photographs for ads, sold advertising space, promoted the *Triangle Business Journal,* and prospected for new advertisers. Summer 1997.

First National Bank, Durham, NC.

Cost-Cutting Analyst. Analyzed existing personal computer allocation and purchasing. Proposed, developed, and instituted cost-cutting measures for existing systems. Implemented technology purchasing procedures. Worked in Consumer Services Group, Country Corporate Office. Summer 1996.

OUTSIDE INTERESTS:

- Northwestern Club Soccer - Treasurer - 1998
- Wayne Manor Selective House - Selection Committee and Social Chairman - 1998
- GALS Little League Softball Coach - 1995 - 1997
- Intramural sports - soccer, basketball, flag football

REFERENCES:

Available upon request.

GEORGE WILLIAM COX

502 Sleigh Street   223 Lindsay Lane
Stockton, CA 95211   Baltimore, MD 21217
(209) 555-2416   (301) 555-2913

EDUCATION

University of the Pacific, Stockton, CA

B.A. Political Science, 2000
GPA: 3.3 on 4.0 scale   Dean's List, 1998 - 1999
Course work: Financial Accounting, Policy Analysis Methods, Statistical Analysis, Managerial
                 Effectiveness, Economics, Calculus, Management and Labor Relations

Summer in Berlin Program, University of the Pacific

Studied German Reformation, Art History

FINANCIAL EXPERIENCE

International Swap Dealers Association, New York, NY

Summer Associate, Summer 1999
                 Reported directly to executive director and senior staff at 200-member
                 international trade association. Conducted extensive research on emerging
                 markets and new derivative products. Planned and organized international
                 swaps conference. Produced historical data trend analysis based on past
                 interest rate and currency swap data.

University of the Pacific Auxiliary Finance Office, Stockton, CA

Senior Accounting Clerk, Summer 1998
                 Reconciled accounts receivable and payable. Collected past-due balances.
                 Researched and responded to vendor inquiries.

Prudential-Bache Securities, Boston, MA

Investment Broker Assistant, Summer 1997
                 Gained strong foundation in fundamental principles and practices of investment
                 decision making. Helped broker analyze and interpret data relating to his clients'
                 accounts.

OTHER EXPERIENCE

University of the Pacific Biology-Forestry Library, Stockton, CA

Library Assistant, Academic years 1997 - 1999
                 Responsible for operation of circulation desk and reserve collections as part of
                 work-study program.

USA TODAY, Arlington, VA

Mail Clerk, Summer 1996
                 Sorted and delivered large volumes of incoming mail. Expedited the requests
                 of top editors and management including rush deliveries and special-
                 handling packages.

INTERESTS   Camping, Fishing, Basketball, Coaching

SKILLS   Proficient in Microsoft Word, Access, Excel, PowerPoint, Web page design.
                 Speak fluent German and French.

REFERENCES   Available upon request.

BRIAN KANEKO

PERMANENT ADDRESS:
57 Rochester Way
Marietta, GA 30060
(404) 555-5445

PRESENT ADDRESS:
P.O. Box 4855
Stanford, CA 94309
(650) 555-1007

OBJECTIVE: An entry-level position in construction management using my technical, organizational, and interpersonal skills to assist with project control tasks.

EDUCATION:

Stanford University, Stanford, CA
Department of Civil Engineering
Master of Science Degree Candidate, May 2000
GPA: 3.2/4.0
Harvey Mudd College, Claremont, CA
School of Civil Environmental Engineering
Bachelor of Science Degree, May 1998
GPA: 3.9/4.0

COURSE WORK:

Civil Engineering Materials, Construction Project Organization and Control, Risk Analysis and Management, Construction Management, Heavy Construction and Earthwork, Legal Aspects of the Construction Process, Decision Analysis in Construction.

EXPERIENCE:

Research Assistant June 1999 - Present
California Transportation Institution, Stockton, CA. Research several design and construction-related areas of bituminous materials as part of the Strategic Highway Research Program, sponsored by the Federal Highway Administration.
Staff Engineer Summers 1997 - 1998
Thompson Engineers, Marietta, GA. Assisted in the preparation of a complete operation and maintenance manual for a leachate treatment plant and provided support in the compilation and review of all operation- and maintenance-related submittals from the general contractor and all subcontractors.

ACHIEVEMENTS:

Engineer-in-Training (EIT) Certification
Dean's List, College of Engineering, Stanford University
Dean's List, College of Engineering, Harvey Mudd College
Graduate Assistantship, Harvey Mudd College

SKILLS: Computer Languages: C/C++, Visual Basic
Computer Applications: Lotus 1-2-3, Excel, SAS, AutoCAD
Fluent in Japanese

REFERENCES: Available upon request.

MARY WU

4838 Mercy Street • Carmel, IN 46032 • (317) 555-2831

OBJECTIVE:
To obtain employment as an accountant.

EDUCATION:
Kalamazoo College, Kalamazoo, MI, 1999
B.A., Economics and Business Administration
GPA 3.75/4.00

COURSE WORK:
Economics, managerial accounting, computer science, calculus, linear algebra, and multivariable calculus

EXPERIENCE:
6/98 - 7/99 **Assistant to Public Relations Director**, United States National Hard Courts, Indianapolis, IN. Typed press releases, updated draw sheets, filed tournament and player data, and answered phones.

Tennis Instructor, Clay Jr. High School, Carmel, IN. Evaluated players, developed lesson plans, and gave group instruction to children and adults.

5/98 - 6/98 **Tennis Camp Instructor and Counselor**, Kalamazoo College, Kalamazoo, MI. Instructed and supervised ranked junior players, organized personal help sessions, and evaluated students.

6/96 - 9/96 **Medical Transcriber**, Dr. Sam Perkins, Family Physician, Carmel, IN. Updated patients' files with information involving diagnosis and treatment, and answered phone calls.

ADDITIONAL
INFORMATION: Taking CPA Examination in Fall 1999.

Junior member of the National Collegiate Athletic Association Division III runner-up varsity tennis team at Kalamazoo College.

Member, Alpha Lambda Delta, a college freshman national honorary society.

REFERENCES: Will be provided upon request.

BEVERLY M. LEBLANC
P.O. Box 8175
Creighton University
Omaha, NE 68178
(402) 555-3686

OBJECTIVE

Environmental engineer position involved with the design of wastewater/water treatment systems, groundwater quality, remediation, groundwater modeling, and hazardous wastes site investigation.

EDUCATION
Creighton University - Omaha, NE
Master of Science in Engineering - 2000
Major: Environmental Engineering
Overall GPA: 3.64/4.00   Major GPA: 3.84/4.00
University of Minnesota - Minneapolis, MN
Bachelor of Science Engineering - 1998
Major: Mechanical Engineering

TECHNICAL SKILLS

- **Major Advanced Courses:**
  Water Quality Analysis, Water Treatment Plant Design, Land Treatment of Wastes, Wastewater Treatment Plant Design, Industrial Wastes Treatment, and Sanitary Engineering.
- **Computer Languages:**   Visual Basic, COBOL MVS
- **Operating Systems:**   MS DOS/MVS; Windows 95, 98, and NT; OS/390
- **Hardware:**   AS 400, OS/390
- **Software:**   Word, SAS, Oracle Database

EXPERIENCE

Fall 1998 - present   **Graduate Research Assistant**
Environmental Engineering Department
Creighton University
Monitoring the operating and treatment efficiency of rotating biological contractors.

Summer 1997   **Programmer**
Environmental Engineering Department
University of Minnesota

Summer 1996   **Operator**
Minneapolis-St. Paul Wastewater Treatment Plant
Minneapolis, MN
Monitored routine operation of facility.

Summer 1995   **Laboratory Analyst**
Science Department
University of Minnesota

ACTIVITIES
- Member of Civil Engineering Honor Society
- Student member of ASCE, WPCF, NSPE

REFERENCES   Will be provided on request.

KELLY JOHNSON
546 Balstrode Way
Des Moines, IA 50312
(515) 555-2376

OBJECTIVE:

To obtain a position working in either a restaurant or drugstore.

EDUCATION:

St. John's High School, 2000
GPA 4.00/4.00
My future educational plans are to attend a four-year state college.

COURSE WORK:

Calculus, Keyboarding, Introduction to Business, and Spanish.

AFFILIATIONS:

Girls High School Swim Team
Interact – A community service club
  Area Representative - Senior
  Vice President - Junior
  Community Commissioner - Sophomore
  Secretary - Freshman

WORK EXPERIENCE:

4/99 - present	**Round Table Pizza.** Cook and Waitress. Assembling pizzas, serving customers and taking their orders, answering phones, and cleaning the restaurant.
6/98 - 8/98	**Prairie Landscapes.** Receptionist. Responsible for answering phones and typing memos.
Weekends	**Baby-sitting**

OTHER EXPERIENCE: Studied Spanish for five years.

OUTSIDE INTERESTS: Reading, playing the piano, and swimming.

REFERENCES: Available upon request.

HEATHER MORENO

48 Hickory Drive
Houston, TX 77002
(713) 555-4968

OBJECTIVE: To obtain a position in the secretarial field.

EDUCATION: Victoria High School, 2000
GPA 3.80/4.00
I plan to attend Texas Southern University and major in business.

COURSE WORK: Keyboarding
Accounting
Mathematics
Introduction to Personal Computers
Psychology

ACTIVITIES: • Council Member of Victoria High School Student Government
• Lead dancer of Flamenco Dance Group
• Organizer of youth group meetings for Christian Fellowship

WORK EXPERIENCE:

6/99 - 12/99   **Patterson Prizes, Inc.**, Receptionist.

Job entailed answering the phone, entering names into a computer, cleaning, and lifting boxes.

INTERESTS: Jogging
Dancing
Reading
Cooking

REFERENCES: Available upon request.

ANTHONY J. RUELAS
364 Sidewinder Way
Lubbock, TX 79409
(806) 555-0923

POSITION DESIRED: Political Aide

EDUCATION:

Lubbock High School, 2000
GPA 3.70/4.00
I plan to attend a four-year university.

COURSE WORK:

Political Science I, II
World History
Computer Science I
Advanced Speech

ACTIVITIES:

A.S.B. President
Student Council, representative
Special Education Community Advisory Committee, member

WORK EXPERIENCE:

OFFICE ASSISTANT, Summer 1999
Network Real Estate
PAGE, September 1998 - February 1999
U.S. House of Representatives

REFERENCES: Upon request

CRISTINA GONZALES
98 Freedom Blvd.
Seattle, WA 98122
(206) 555-4691

**POSITION
DESIRED:**   A salaried community service position
enabling me to work with and help others.

EDUCATION: Seattle High School, 2000
GPA 3.50/4.00, four-year member of honor society.

I plan to attend a four-year university to obtain a
degree in psychology.

**SCHOOL
ACTIVITIES:**   Sophomore class president
A.S.B. member
Commissioner of Hospitality
Soccer team member
Softball team member

**OUTSIDE
INTERESTS:**   Writing
Soccer
Softball
Reading
Swimming

SKILLS: Able to speak fluent Spanish.
Type 40 words per minute.

**WORK
EXPERIENCE:**   **Wal-Mart**, Seattle, WA
Merchandise cashier
5-98 to 9-00

REFERENCES: Available upon request.

NATHAN MOYA

---

562 York Ave. South • Beaverton, OR 97005 • (503) 555-4159

GOAL:

To display my diligent work ethic while gaining solid work experience.

EDUCATION:

Beaverton High School, 2000
GPA 3.50/4.00
I plan to attend a four-year university and law school.

COURSE WORK:

Leadership class - organization, leadership, responsibility
Geometry - abstract thinking
Spanish - fluency in another language

ACTIVITIES:

Swim Team
Track-and-Field Team
Student Trustee to the School Board
Member - Associated Student Body
Boy Scouts Life Rank
Volunteer - AIDS Quilt, 1999
Volunteer - Food Bank, 1998

INTERESTS:

Swimming
Backpacking
Running
Hiking
Cycling

SKILLS:

Fluent in the Spanish language
Computer literate - Macintosh and Windows 98

**WORK
EXPERIENCE:**

McDonald's   Summer 2000.   Efficiently served customers with a positive attitude
Ed's Upholstery 1998 - 1999. Dependably picked up and delivered furniture, cleaned shop

REFERENCES: Available on request.

Marybeth A. Whittle
5679 Opal Cliff
Edmonds, WA 98020
(206) 555-2177

GOAL

To obtain a position in which I can demonstrate my ability
to handle challenging tasks.

EDUCATION

Edmonds High School, 2000
GPA 3.80/4.00
Next year I will be attending Georgetown University.
After completing my college education, I plan to enter law school.

SCHOOL ACTIVITIES

Cheerleading
Associated Student Body - Secretary
Site Council Member
Key Club - Community service club member

WORK EXPERIENCE

Jennifer's Bakery - cash register, cleaning
Summers 1998, 1999

INTERESTS

Running
Knitting

PERSONAL

I am a responsible individual who enjoys working with others.

REFERENCES

Available upon request.

ELIZABETH M. LEIGH-WOOD

387 Sunny Hills Drive
Madison, WI 53711
(608) 555-1524

OBJECTIVE	*A position as a lifeguard. I am certified in Standard First Aid and CPR and have passed a lifeguard training course.*
EDUCATION	• Madison High School, 2000 GPA 3.80/4.00 • General education/Honors classes • Next year I will be attending Cardinal Stritch University in Milwaukee, WI, on a track scholarship.
SCHOOL ACTIVITIES	• Four-year Member of Associated Student Body Council • Four-year Member of Wisconsin Scholarship Federation • Four-year Member of Varsity Track Team • Two-year Member of Varsity Swim Team
ACTIVITIES	• 1999 - 2000: Hospital Volunteer • 1998 - 2000: American Cancer Society Volunteer Christmas Gift Wrapper
SKILLS	• Fluent in French • Hardworking and outgoing
WORK EXPERIENCE	• Whalers' Car Wash, 5/99 - 10/99 • Lifeguard, Sunny Hills Neighborhood Club, 5/98 - 8/98 • Baby-sitting, weekends
REFERENCES	Upon request.

SERENA STRELITZ

645 Doris Avenue • Salt Lake City, UT 84112 • (801) 555-0211

OBJECTIVE: I am seeking a job in sales, either clothing or food.

EDUCATION: Salt Lake City High School, 2000
GPA 4.25/4.00
General education/Honors and Advanced Placement classes
I will be attending Brigham Young University, Provo, UT,
during the following academic year. I plan to obtain a
master's degree in Communication.

SKILLS:
- Fluent in Spanish
- Hardworking
- Congenial worker

WORK
EXPERIENCE: Work in the **Farm Bakery** - salesperson.
November 1998 to present.
Worked in the **Snack Shack** at football games -
salesperson, cashier, and cook.
August to October, 1996 to 1999.

SCHOOL
ACTIVITIES:
- Three-year member of Interact, a Community Service Club
- Three-year member of Key Club, a Community Service Club
- Four-year member of Utah Scholarship Federation,
  including one year as President
- Two-year member of Varsity Track Team

VOLUNTEER
WORK:
- I have spent one year as an assistant in a first grade class, 1999.
- I worked in a political campaign to elect a state representative in 1998.

REFERENCES: Available upon request.

MATTHEW BERDAL

351 Huntington Drive
Jacksonville, FL 32211
(904) 555-5050

GOAL:
A position using my skills as a specialist in PC software training and network support.

QUALIFICATIONS:
Expert troubleshooter and problem solver.
Proven ability to educate and motivate others.
Proficient in PC software and hardware.

EDUCATION:
Jacksonville University, Jacksonville, FL - 2000
Major - Computer Science   GPA 3.8/4.0

TRAINING:
• Visual Basic
• Programming
• DEC - PCSA/VAX Based Server System Management
• DEC - Network Management I
• DEC - VAX/VMS System Management I

EMPLOYMENT
HISTORY:
INFO TEC Video Systems, Jacksonville, FL
PC Specialist, 1998 - present
Programmer, 1997

BOB'S Family Market, Jacksonville, FL
Manager, 1996

PROFESSIONAL
EXPERIENCE:
• Acted as administrator for ALL-IN-1 electronic mail on a VAX 4000, with the integration of PC word-processing documents and spreadsheets.
• Repaired and upgraded all components of PC hardware: Compaq, AST, IBM, AT&T, HP, Epson, Dell, and Gateway.
• Provided technical consulting to managers demonstrating comprehensive awareness of staff needs.
• Trained PC users nationwide via telephone.
• Instructed company personnel on an individual basis.
• Designed and presented training classes on PC software, DOS, and PC fundamentals.

REFERENCES: Available upon request.

CARLOS RAMIREZ

529 Venetian Way Augusta, ME 04330   (207) 555-6053

OBJECTIVE: *To obtain a position in management or finance.*

EDUCATION: *Harvard Graduate School of Business Administration,*
M.B.A., 2000
Columbia University, B.A. Economics, 1995

COMPUTER
EXPERIENCE: *Programs and Software: WordPerfect and Microsoft Word,*
Computer-Assisted Design and Drafting, and
Statistical Analysis System
Hardware: IBM, HP, Dell, Gateway, and Macintosh

PROFESSIONAL
EXPERIENCE:
Summer 1999   PITTMAN EQUITIES CORPORATION, Augusta, ME
Investment Processor

Responsible for operation of personal computer systems, design and preparation of company sales reports and financial reports, and design of the company's databases using Personal Decision Series software.

1995 - 1998   McCORMICK COMPANY, New York, NY
Manager and Director of Investment Services

Managed all aspects of a 40-node 3Com 3Plus local-area network, including software configuration and installation, user maintenance, file maintenance, backup procedures, and all day-to-day operations. Responsibilities included portfolio analysis and account management in Investment Services Department.

AWARDS: *• Harvard University - Baker Scholar*
• Phi Beta Kappa - 1995

INTERESTS: *Traveling, waterskiing, and reading.*

REFERENCES: *Available upon request.*

MARVIN HOPKINS

341 Beach Pines Drive • Olympia, WA 98505 • (206) 555-2397

OBJECTIVE

To work as a project engineer with a computer manufacturer and advance to a management position in research and development.

EDUCATION

Eastern Washington University, Cheney, WA
B.S. Computer and Information Sciences, 2000

TECHNICAL SUMMARY

Software: Lotus 1-2-3, WordPerfect, TCP/IP, Microsoft Office
                  (Excel, PowerPoint, Word, Access), and Windows Explorer.

Hardware: Windows-compatible personal computers, Macintosh computers,
                  laser/inkjet printers, modems, plotters, scanners, and AS/400.

Languages: Visual Basic, COBOL MVS, DB2, Oracle Databases, and SQL.

SUMMER WORK EXPERIENCE

1998 - 1999   Microsoft - Redmond, WA
                  Assistant Systems Manager - Member of four-person team that installed and implemented a 60-node 3Com 3Plus local area network, including 53 IBM-compatible personal computers and 9 Macintosh computers. Provided support for WordPerfect, Lotus 1-2-3, and electronic mail.

                  MCCAW Cellular Communications - Kirkland, WA
                  Programmer and Educator - Provided support for all aspects of IBM-compatible personal computers, including software.

REFERENCES

Work and education references on request.

Willing to relocate.

Sarah Louise Hill
865 Woodside Drive
Chattanooga, TN 37403
(615) 555-0469

PROFESSIONAL OBJECTIVE:

To gain a position as a marketing representative with possibility of advancement into management position.

EDUCATION:

UNIVERSITY OF TENNESSEE
Chattanooga, TN
B.S., Business Administration, anticipated May 2001

EXPERIENCE:

Summers 1999, 2000

UNION PLANTERS CORPORATION OF AMERICA
Nashville, TN
Sales Representative: Responsible for service and sales in the Nashville area. Increased sales by 5 percent each summer. Awarded the 1999 Murphy's Trophy for achieving sales expectancy in every product line.

Summer 1998

HEALTHTRUST
Nashville, TN
Sales Representative: Achieved 150 percent expected quota for June to August calling on business and industrial accounts in Tennessee. Ranked #1 out of 12 salespeople.

Summer 1997

A & P SUPERMARKET
Nashville, TN
Cashier

COMPUTER EXPERIENCE:

Word, Access, Excel

HOBBIES AND INTERESTS:

Golf, softball, family activities, travel, volunteer work

REFERENCES:

References will be provided upon request.

Willing to relocate.

RACHEL DURAN

298 Cass Street
Salem, OR 97309
(503) 555-5329

P.O. Box 1048
Eugene, OR 97405
(503) 555-5917

OBJECTIVE

To serve as a receptionist in the executive suite of a large corporation.

EDUCATION

Lane Community College, Eugene, OR, 2000
Degree - Business and Office Technician

ACHIEVEMENTS

Lane Community College Dean's List, December 1999
Lane Community College "Student of the Month," October 1999
Certificates of Achievement for accounting, English, and spelling
Oregon Girls State Representative, 1995
Student Body Treasurer, Salem High School, 1995 - 1996
Who's Who on the West Coast, 1996 ed.

SKILLS

Computer: MS Word, Access
Machine transcription
Typing, 85 wpm

EXPERIENCE

RECEPTIONIST - U.S. BANKCORP, Portland, OR, Summers 1998, 1999.
Job included: typing, filing, and processing mail.

RECEPTIONIST - William H. Schmeida M.D., Salem, OR, Summer 1997.
Job included: handling monthly reports, typing, processing mail,
and filing general correspondence material.

REFERENCES

Available upon request.

NOLAN T. YU

Present Address:	P.O. Box 61434 Cambridge, MA 02139 (617) 555-6087
Permanent Address:	1534 Elm Street Catonsville, MD 21228 (301) 555-6053

Objective: To obtain a position in finance or consulting that requires technical expertise.

Education: MASSACHUSETTS INSTITUTE OF TECHNOLOGY, Cambridge, MA
B.S. Computer and Information Sciences
June 2000   GPA: 3.5/4.0

Experience: MIT BOOKSTORE
Loss Prevention Agent
Coordinated shrinkage control system, which included the compilation of monthly reports on loss prediction data and statistics. Division reduced inventory loss due to theft by 12 percent. (2/00 - 6/00)

MIT DINING SOCIETY
Financial Manager
Coordinated a quarterly budget of $65,000. Investigated and analyzed budgetary problems. Revised financial accounting system and established mechanisms for the analysis of fiscal progress through implementation of a database management software system. (9/98 - 6/99)

Skills: PC and Macintosh: Windows 2000; Mac S9.0; MS Office: Excel, Word, Access, Outlook Express
Fluent in Chinese (Mandarin)

Additional Information: MIT Engineering Association
MIT Pre-business Society
Varsity tennis team, 1997 - 1998

References available upon request.

LORETTA M. ALSTON

305 Doris Avenue
Baldwin City, KS 66006
(913) 555-0211

OBJECTIVE   To obtain a position in which my secretarial skills, ability to organize, and willingness to assume responsibility can be employed.

EDUCATION   Baker University; Baldwin City, KS, 2000
Major: English Literature

EXPERIENCE
Summers
1998 - 1999   REINHARDT & ASSOCIATES LAW CORPORATION
Baldwin City, KS
Personal Secretary for Michael J. Green
• Composed and prepared correspondence
• Handled accounts receivable
• Performed receptionist and general secretarial duties

Summer
1997   SPEEDO INC.
Baldwin City, KS
Secretary
• Performed data entry on PC
• Maintained mailing list database
• Purchased office supplies

Summers
1995 - 1996   EXECUTIVE SUNN CENTERS
Baldwin City, KS
Receptionist

ADDITIONAL
INFORMATION   I am familiar with these computer programs: Microsoft Windows 98, Microsoft Office 2000, and WordPerfect.
I can type 81 words per minute.

REFERENCES   Available upon request.

CHARLES P. BHATIA

Campus Address: Permanent Address:

P.O. Box 7327	234 Rose Street
Henniker, NH 03242	Greenville, IL 62246
(603) 555-7123	(618) 555-4335

Objective   To obtain a position in manufacturing, analysis, or project development.

Education   *New England College,* Henniker, NH.
Pursuing B.S. in Industrial Engineering, June 2001. GPA: 3.5/4.0.
Responsible for 20 percent of college expenses.

Experience

6/00 - 9/00   **Management Engineering Intern**
Greenville Health Center, Greenville, IL.
Analyzed work flow and made recommendations to hospital administrator. Built computerized daily productivity report and employee database file converters. Led team in continuous process improvement project, which involved extensive interviewing.

1/98 - 6/99   **Student Manager**
Bon Appetit, Henniker, NH.
Interviewed and trained new and current employees. Scheduled workers and reduced labor costs significantly. Planned strategies with director of retail. Changed and improved products. Inventoried and ordered food products weekly. Served and cashiered.

Activities

8/99 5/00   **Student Government Association Member**
Henniker, NH.
Coordinated survey of 2,000 undergraduate classes as assistant director of course evaluations. Debated proposed legislation as the representative for the undergraduate academic council. Oversaw student election process on the ethics committee.

9/97 - 6/00   **Team/Urban Community Vision/Community Volunteer**
Henniker, NH.
Tutored underprivileged children weekly at their schools. Programmed children's retreat.

Computer Skills
Computer knowledge includes SAS, WordPerfect, Lotus 1-2-3, Excel, Access, programming in C/C++.

References   Available upon request.

VICTORIA ALEXANDER FLYNN

ADDRESS   4678 Freedom Blvd.
             Newark, Delaware 19716

TELEPHONE (302) 555-4780

CAREER OBJECTIVE
A growth-oriented position in Human Resources Management

EDUCATION
University of Delaware, Newark, DE
Master's in Business Administration, 2000
Goldey Beacom College, Wilmington, DE
B.S., Business and Management, 1998

SUMMER EXPERIENCE
1998 and 1999

KELSEY TECHNOLOGIES CORPORATION
Member of team whose responsibilities included
- Contingency plan development/implementation
- Administration of various salaried benefit programs
- Hourly and salaried technical training
- Salary planning

1996 and 1997

NEWARK PUBLIC SCHOOLS
Teacher's aide whose responsibilities included
- Instruction of business law, business management, and accounting to high school juniors and seniors
- Curriculum development

ADDITIONAL INFORMATION
Excellent skills in MS Word and Access
Four Varsity Letters in field hockey, Goldey Beacom College
Three Varsity Letters in track and field, Goldey Beacom College
Assistant coach, Wilmington High School field hockey team

REFERENCES
Available upon request

PHILIP E. GADBAW

1625 South Sylvester Street   P.O. Box 9087
Crestview Hills, KY 41017   Bowling Green, KY 42101
(606) 555-2368   (502) 555-9850

OBJECTIVE: A position in product/brand marketing offering exposure to product
                 planning and development, market research, and advertising.

EDUCATION: Master of Business Administration, May 2000
                 Western Kentucky University
                 GPA 4.00/4.00
                 A broad graduate program in marketing and finance, supported by
                 course work in management, business planning, operations, econom-
                 ics, and accounting.

                 Bachelor of Science degree in Industrial Engineering, May 1998
                 Glenville State College
                 Extensive course work in economics, mathematics, statistics, and com-
                 munications art.

EXPERIENCE: Liberty National Bancorp   Louisville, KY
                 Summers 1998, 1999

                 Industrial Engineer
                 Designing, performing, and presenting factory and office productivity
                 studies with measured savings in excess of $200,000 per study. Accom-
                 plishments include the successful engineering, organizing, and pre-
                 senting of projects and layouts involving expenditures up to $300,000.

                 Humana   Louisville, KY
                 Summer 1997

                 Packaging Engineer
                 Initiated cost savings for June - August period.

                 Circuit City Stores   Glenville, WV
                 Summer 1996

                 Engineering Internship
                 Responsibilities included routing, structuring of bill of materials, and
                 supervising hourly employees.

REFERENCES: Available upon request.

CRAIG L. HJORRING

31 Anderson Road • Fort Collins, CO 80523 • (303) 555-0469

OBJECTIVE

Management position with special emphasis in Marketing and Sales.

EDUCATION

Colorado State University, Fort Collins, CO
B.S. in Business Administration and Management expected May 2001
GPA 3.49/4.00

MEMBERSHIPS

Society of Manufacturing Engineers
Fabricating Manufacturers Association

EXPERIENCE

Sutherland Sports Wear
Assistant Regional Sales Manager
Summers 1998 - 2000

ACHIEVEMENTS

Orchestrated and created all sales literature and advertising, which decreased advertising costs from 8.5 percent to 2.4 percent of sales.

Increased sales from June to August more than 20 percent each summer.

Acquired industry contacts providing for joint ventures with suppliers and customers as member of sales team.

PERSONAL

I enjoy biking, swimming, and family activities.

REFERENCES

Available upon request.

CHRISTOPHER J. HEALY

142 Peachtree Lane
Montgomery, AL 36193
(205) 555-9484

OBJECTIVE   *To obtain a position within a marketing or general management firm.*

EDUCATION   **FAULKNER UNIVERSITY,** Montgomery, AL - 2000
Associate degree in Business Administration
and Management
Bachelor's degree in Accounting
GPA 4.00/4.00

HONORS   Beta Gamma Sigma
Business/Management Honorary
Accounting Honorary

**PART-TIME WORK
EXPERIENCE**   **Head Coach for Montgomery Summer Basketball League.**
Organized and directed four winning teams, including
Sectional and Cluster Champions.
June to August, 1998 and 1999

Assistant Coach for Montgomery Summer Basketball League.
June to August, 1997

Waiter at Max's Grill. Primarily served food,
occasionally helped to clean and clear tables.
June to August, 1994, 1995, and 1996

REFERENCES   Furnished upon request.

NICOLE ANNE CHANG

Address:
3089 McGlenn Drive
Jonesboro, AR 72402   (501) 555-9268

OBJECTIVE: Position as a veterinarian assistant, 30 to 35 hours per week.

EDUCATION: Arkansas State University, Jonesboro, AR - 2000
B.S. in Biology
GPA - 3.45/4.00

AWARDS: Member of Dean's List - 2000
All-Academic Soccer Team - 1999
High School All-American Soccer Player - 1996

EXPERIENCE: Veterinarian Assistant Volunteer, Michael Stein's Veterinary
Hospital. June to August, 1998 and 1999

Assisted with the administration of medicine and pacification
of the animals.

Assistant Coach, Jonesboro Summer Soccer League.
June 5 to July 31, 1996 to 1999

PERSONAL:

I am a very patient and caring person.
I love working with animals.
I am willing to relocate.

References on request.

CHRISTOPHER M. ISEBRAND
2711 Mar Vista Drive
Farmington, CT 06032
(203) 555-8900

OBJECTIVE

A position as a technician or an assembler.

BACKGROUND SUMMARY

Have demonstrated analytical, technical, and managerial skills. Communicate effectively with corporate representatives and government inspectors. Able to think in an objective manner. Possess excellent problem-solving skills. Work habits are clean and organized.

EDUCATION

U.S. Navy
Avionics Electronics classes (equivalent to A.A. Degree)

Central Connecticut State University, New Britain, CT, 1985
B.S., Engineering Technology
Minor - Manufacturing Technology
GPA - 3.56/4.00

EXPERIENCE

U.S. Navy, Aviation Electrician, 1985 - 2000
Received an Honorable Discharge.

PERSONAL

I have lived in Hawaii and Japan.

REFERENCES

Available upon request.

MELISSA L. JUNG
1530 Hansen Lane
Dover, DE 19901
(302) 555-9401

OBJECTIVE: To secure employment as an elementary education teacher.

EDUCATION: University of Delaware, Newark, DE - 1979
                        M.A., Education

                        Wesley College, Dover, DE - 1977
                        B.A., Elementary Education
                        GPA 3.90/4.00

VOLUNTEER
EXPERIENCE: Assistant art teacher, *Dover Elementary School.*

                        Five-year member *Dover Rotary Club*.
                        Head of fund-raiser to finance a new local elementary school.
                        Raised $54,000.

                        Volunteer at local homeless soup kitchen every Wednesday evening.

                        Hostess for six exchange students from France, Germany, and Japan.

PERSONAL: Homemaker 1980 - present.

                        Mother of four children.

                        I assist my husband in his business, delivering merchandise,
                        purchasing supplies, and arranging financing.

                        I enjoy swimming, biking, and traveling.

REFERENCES: Available upon request.

LARRY LAWSON JONES

6542 Jackson Blvd.
La Mesa, CA 91941
(619) 555-3428

EMPLOYMENT OBJECTIVE

A career in aviation beginning as airplane pilot of a commercial single/twin engine.

SUMMARY

Graduate of the University of California, Irvine, with Bachelor of Arts degree in Economics. Supplemented a challenging academic program with flying and sailing. Received a private pilot license as a personal goal and competed in college sailing.

EDUCATION

Aeronautical

- American Flyers, San Diego, CA, Instrument Rating, October 2000.
- Sunrise Aviation, Orange County, CA, Private Pilot's License, December 1999.

General

- University of California, Irvine
  B.A. Economics, June 2000.

HONORS

- Nominee, Scholar-Athlete, University of California, Irvine, 2000.
- Collegiate All-American sailor, 1999, 2000.

EXPERIENCE

Aeronautical

- 240 hours, much of it complex, including transcontinental flights.
- Working on commercial rating now.

General

- Sailing Coach, University High School, San Diego, CA, 1998 - 2000.
- Yacht racing clinic instructor for San Diego Yacht Club, 1998 - 1999.
- Represented USA at Japan/USA Goodwill Regatta, Tokyo, Japan, 1998.

REFERENCES

Will be made available on request.

HOWARD LUM
125 Apple Lane
Daytona Beach, FL 32015
(904) 555-8875

OBJECTIVE

A position in residential or commercial construction.

EDUCATION

Broward Community College, Fort Lauderdale, FL - 2000
Major - Landscape Architecture
GPA 2.94/4.00

Daytona Beach High School, Daytona Beach, FL - 1998
Business course
GPA 3.44/4.00

PART-TIME WORK EXPERIENCE

June to August, 1996 to 1999
Florida State Insulation Co. - Daytona Beach, FL
Started as a laborer and worked up to the position of assistant foreman of a five-man crew. Responsible for previewing jobs, supplying material, and performing residential and commercial insulation applications.

June to September 1995
Simmons Roofing Company - Daytona Beach, FL
Performed all phases of hot asphalt and shingle roofing on both commercial and residential properties.

PERSONAL

I am a very diligent and hardworking individual who has the ability to give and receive directions effectively.

My hobbies include mountain climbing and skiing.

REFERENCES

Are available upon request.

MAXWELL Y. KITYAMA
4200 Birch Lane • Rome, GA 30163
(404) 555-5450

OBJECTIVE

Full-time employment as a mechanic.

EXPERIENCE

BUTLER MACHINERY, Rome, GA   **Summers 1997 to 2000**
Manufacturer of correct mechanical components for high technology.

Set up the operation of machine tools, including lathes, milling machines, drill presses, and grinders. Experienced with precision measuring instruments; fabrication procedures including welding, sheet metal, and casting; and interpretation of documentation conventions for dimensions, tolerance, and finishing.

PERSONAL

I am skilled in mechanics, carpentry, masonry, painting, and landscaping.
I enjoy playing golf and baseball.
I am a volunteer coach for the local high school baseball summer league team.

EDUCATION

Floyd College, Rome, GA
A.S. Mechanical Engineering, 2000

Rome High School, Rome, GA
Specialty - Mechanics, 1998

REFERENCES

Full references will be furnished on request.

ROBERTO I. MARTINEZ

1690 Sandy Lane • Marianna, FL 34619 • (813) 555-7758

JOB OBJECTIVE

Technician/Assistant Engineer
Industrial/Production Electronics

A position offering upward mobility in a quiet, professional environment. I am confident I can adapt successfully to the industrial/production environment and as a self-starter, I will learn whatever additional skills the position requires.

PART-TIME WORK EXPERIENCE

Summer occupation 1997 to 1999 - Marianna Radio/TV, Marianna, FL
TV, VCR, and Stereo Technician.

Summer occupation 1996 - Allen TV Service, Marianna, FL
TV/Stereo Technician.

Summer occupation 1995 - McDonald's restaurant, Marianna, FL
Food Server and Maintenance Worker.

PERSONAL EVALUATION

I am an electronics technician with a strong background in repairing consumer electronic products. I have designed and breadboarded many electronic devices such as TTL circuits up to 14 ICs, audio special-effects projects, laser and power supply projects, security systems, infrared and ultrasonic measuring tools, and surface mount technology projects.

EDUCATION

2000 Graduate of Chipola Junior College, Marianna, FL

A.A. Equivalence Certificates in Electronics, AC/DC, Semiconductors, Circuits, Digital Electronics, and Microprocessors.

1998 Graduate of Marianna High School, Marianna, FL
General education.

REFERENCES ON REQUEST

EMILIA E. ALDRICH
1609 Poppy Way
Franklin Springs, GA 30639
(404) 555-0155

OBJECTIVE:

A position in sales with opportunity to reach the managerial level.

PERSONAL:

I always make an effort to complete scheduled projects successfully and on time.

I am eager to learn and attentive to quality.

I enjoy mountain biking, cooking, and fishing.

EXPERIENCE:

City Market, Franklin Springs, GA. Checker/Stock Clerk. Duties included ordering of groceries and supplies, stocking shelves, cashiering, making weekly deposits to checking account, recording and submitting welfare vouchers, and taking inventory. Summers 1997, 1998, and 1999.

EDUCATION:

2000 Graduate of Emmanuel College, Franklin Springs, GA

GPA 3.23/4.00

Major - Business and Office Studies

1998 Graduate of Franklin Springs High School

Educational focus on business courses.

REFERENCES:

Available.

ROSAMARIA C. ALVAREZ
255 Outlook Drive
Twin Falls, ID 83303
(208) 555-3242

OBJECTIVE   A position as a senior or supervising receptionist providing efficient, high-quality typing, clerical, and word processing services to a business firm.

EDUCATION   College of Southern Idaho - 1999
• Certificate in Business Practices
• Typing: 80 WPM
• Office practice
• Business machines

EXPERIENCE   *Manpower Temporary Services, Twin Falls, ID*
June to August 1996, 1997, and 1998
General office worker.
• Filed applications, greeted applicants, and answered phones.
• Assisted with administration and grading of applicants' tests and completed all test paperwork.
• Gained experience in light invoicing, setting up files, typing, and data entry.

Idaho State Automobile Association, Twin Falls, ID
June to August 1995.
Assistant cashier, relief PBX, and relief DMV.
• Assisted customers with paperwork.
• Entered data in computer system.

COMPUTER
EXPERIENCE   • Windows 98
• Microsoft Office 2000
• WordPerfect
• NEC PowerMate 8100 Series
• Microsoft Excel
• Microsoft PowerPoint

REFERENCES   Available upon request.

CARRIE KING
704 Timberlake Court
Clinton, IA 52732
(319) 555-1466

Objective
A full-time position as clerical assistant with possibility of advancement.

Education	Clinton Community College, Clinton, IA Associate's degree, 2000
Course Work	• Microsoft Word 2000 • Microsoft Publishing • Drafting • Real Estate • "Filing Efficiently" seminar • "Take Charge Secretary" seminar
Experience	**AEC Communications,** Clinton, IA Part-Time Receptionist. 1998 - present 4 hours/day • Greet people and answer multilined telephone. • Support office staff. **The Midwest Consumer,** Clinton, IA Personal Assistant. 1997 - summer • Assisted applicants and new employees with paperwork. • Handled general office duties including the filing. • Assisted payroll occasionally. • Kept notes of committee meetings. • Assisted personnel manager with tasks including screening applicants and interviewing. *References will be provided upon request.*

KEVIN R. LEE

46 La Mesa Drive

Coffeyville, KS 67337

(316) 555-1058

Summary:_____

Technician experienced in assembly of electromechanical devices pertinent to cathode ray tubes. Experienced with soldering, welding, cleaning, and leak detection equipment. Familiar with most laboratory operations and tools including conformance to process specifications and collecting/organizing data.

Education:_____

11/98 - 11/99   **Coffeyville Control Data Institute** - Coffeyville, KS

Completed 853-hour course in computer technology. Studies included basic and advanced electronics, digital logic and circuit analysis, Boolean algebra, CDC-Cyber 18-20 central processor, the 8080 microprocessor, hardware and software, peripheral equipment including card equipment, line printer, magnetic tape transport, and magnetic disc drive. Twenty percent hands-on time. Course also included extensive use of dual-trace oscilloscope multi-meter logic trainers and visual display devices.

Experience:_____

4/97 - 10/98   **Mendelson Corporation** - Coffeyville, KS
                   Test Technician

Tested and troubleshot a model 340 and a model 390 spectrophotometer. Performed tests on printed circuit boards and subassemblies.

Summers
1995, 1996   **Your Market** - Coffeyville, KS
                   Checker/Stock Clerk

Ordered groceries and supplies, cashiered, made weekly deposits to checking account, took inventory, stocked shelves, recorded and submitted food stamp vouchers.

References: Available upon your request.

Sophia L. Krook

Address:

746 Pineview Drive
Frederick, MD 21701
(301) 555-3121

Objective:

To use my education and experience in a challenging position in computer-based technical or customer support, with potential for advancement.

Education:

George Washington University, Washington, D.C.
B.A. Anthropology, 1987, with emphasis in advertising
GPA 4.00/4.00

Awards:

1999 Matt Arnerich Community Service Award
George Washington University Honors,
Outstanding Academic Achievement, 1987

Areas of Expertise:

I have the ability to combine a high level of customer relations and organizational skills with a sound analytical knowledge of technical line production and troubleshooting. I am computer literate in production and diagnostic testing using Hewlett Packard computers, frequency counters, spectrum analyzers, network analyzers, and power meters among others.

Skills:

I have self-taught PC familiarity and am well-versed in Windows. I am skilled in Visual Basic, Word, Oracle Database, and TCP/IP. Also, I am active on many bulletin boards and familiar with shareware and freeware in many categories.

References Available Upon Request

Sabrina K. Lara
40065 Early Way
Boise, ID 83725
(208) 555-9203

Objective   A position as a personal office executive.

Education   Boise State University, 1993 - 1994
    Nine units toward Management Certificate
     • Personnel Management
     • Basic Supervision
     • Computers in Management
    Professional office training (14 units)
     • Business English, Math, and Machines
     • Office Procedures
     • Refresher Typing and Shorthand
   Other
    Accounting Principles (6 units)
    Seminars relating to the personnel field
     • Wage and Salary Administration
     • Hiring and Firing
     • EEOC Compliance

Skills   Work well with people. Excellent writing and organizational skills.
   Flexible and patient. Enjoy creative projects.

Interests   Reading, music (play flute and piano)
   Traveling and learning about other cultures

Experience Self-Employed
   Assist in the publication of a monthly newsletter, *The Quaker Trails,* and a
   quarterly one, *Let's Talk About Real Estate*. Developed marketing materials
   for a realtor, including "Career Portfolio," and a "Marketing Booklet" used to
   market individual listings.

References will be provided upon request.

SIWA MSANGI

2590 Atlas Drive
Cedar Rapids, IA 52402
(319) 555-5850

OBJECTIVE

Full-time executive secretary appointment with potential for advancement to personal assistant.

EDUCATION

Coe College - Cedar Rapids, IA
Bachelor of Arts, 1992
Major - Music
Minor - Art History and Appreciation
GPA 3.5/4.0

Cedar Rapids High School - 1988
Educational emphasis in theater and music

VOLUNTEER HISTORY

1993 - 2000   Des Moines Symphony Orchestra
                     Executive Secretary to President and Music Director

                     Provided administrative assistance. Prepared agendas and minutes
                     of Board and Executive Committee meetings and scheduled
                     meetings for fiscal year. Attended meetings for President.
                     Maintained business and social calendars. Composed and
                     transcribed correspondence. Supervised volunteers for special
                     projects.

REFERENCES

Will be furnished upon request.

PENNIE L. PORTER _____
1730 Cowper Street
Parsons, KS 67357
(913) 555-9430

Objective: A position that will provide me with opportunities to learn and
                   advance professionally.

Education: Labette Community College, Parsons, KS
                   Associate's degree in Computer and Information Sciences, 1994
                   Parsons High School, 1992

Skills and Experience:

Low Land Computer   1992 - 2000

As a volunteer in the family company, I have become experienced in all aspects of the
processing of domestic shipments.

- Used UPS, Federal Express, and Airborne Express meter machines and
  Pitney Bowes U.S. Mail meter to dispatch and expedite truck shipments.

- Processed international shipments.

- Recorded and controlled all parts incoming and outgoing of the finished goods
  inventory.

- Performed data entry.

- Recorded supplies used in the traffic department and created purchase orders.

McDonald's   Summers 1991 - 1993

As opening cook, I became familiar with the process of making fast food.

- Prepared food to order.

- Restocked supplies to be used for the day.

References will be provided upon request.

LAURA KIRSTEN HUMMEL

529 Paul Revere Drive
Longmeadow, MA 01160
(413) 555-3093

OBJECTIVE: **A part-time job that will allow me to support myself while attending culinary school.**

EDUCATION: **2000 Graduate of Longmeadow High School**
My scholastic GPA was 3.1/4.0.

FUTURE PLANS: **I will attend Bay Path College and study food preparation and other culinary skills. I then plan to attend a university and major in restaurant management.**

EXPERIENCE: **The past three summers I have worked at *Charlie's Deli Cafe* in Longmeadow, MA. My duties included taking food orders, checking stock, preparing food, and operating the cash register.**

PERSONAL: **I was a two-year member of Longmeadow High's German Club.**

I was a cheerleader at Longmeadow High for four years.

I am hardworking and dedicated.

TRANSPORTATION: **I own a 1990 Mazda truck that can be used for transportation and work if necessary.**

REFERENCES: **Jay Johnson, Teacher, Longmeadow High School, (413) 555-0711.**

Mary Hicks, Coach, Longmeadow High School, (413) 555-0711.

Mitch L. DeLorenzo
29 Alta Drive
Fulton, MS 38843
(601) 555-0331

Objective   I am very interested in obtaining employment that allows me to
                continually progress toward higher levels of performance. I am easily
                trained, a responsible employee, and a pleasant person to work with.

Education   I graduated from Fulton High School in 2000. My studies were
                concentrated in economics and business.

                I have always been very active in sports. While at Fulton High School, I
                participated on the following athletic teams:
                        Soccer team (4 years; 2 years varsity).
                        Track and cross-country team (3 years).
                        Swim team (1 year).

                I was the financial manager during my senior year of the varsity soccer
                team. This position taught me how to combine work and play.

                I plan to attend Itawamba Community College for the next 2 years
                where my studies will focus on business economics.

Experience   Joseph's Motor Home Service and Repair, Fulton, MS
                June 1, 1999, to September 1, 1999

                I was responsible for washing and repairing recreational vehicles. My job
                also included installing new accessories and appliances in motor homes.

References   Joseph Goode
                Joseph's Motor Home Service and Repair
                (601) 555-8965

WILLIAM R. TANIMOTO
780 Weston Road
Mathiston, MS 39752
(601) 555-4194

OBJECTIVE: A position as a part-time chef for the next two years with potential for full-time position after graduation from college.

EDUCATION: Graduate of Mathiston High School, 2000
GPA 2.80/4.00
I plan to attend Wood Junior College in Mathiston, MS, starting fall 2000.

PERSONAL: Four-year member of the Mathiston High School baseball team.

Two-year member of the Adopt-a-Grandparent program at the Convalescent Hospital in Mathiston.

Reliable and ready to work.

EXPERIENCE:

Summers   **JACOB'S RIB COMPANY, Mathiston, MS**
1996 - 2000   **Cook and Food Preparations**
- Cooking
- Operating cash register
- Preparing food backups
- Bussing tables
- Counting the money in the cash register drawer

REFERENCES: Will be made available upon request.

REBECCA C. PALMER

ADDRESS   345 Kingsbury Drive
                           Hillsboro, MO 63050

TELEPHONE   (314) 555-8832

PROFESSIONAL
OBJECTIVE   A permanent position as a receptionist or secretary in a
                           well-established company with good benefits and
                           opportunities for advancement

EDUCATION   Hillsboro High School - 2000

COURSE WORK   Shorthand   two semesters
                           Keyboarding   two semesters
                           Record Keeping   one semester
                           Business Math   one semester

EXPERIENCE   Summer 1999
                           Wendy's
                           Crew Person:
                                Took customer orders
                                Cooked
                                Helped close the restaurant

REFERENCES   Available upon request

ANTHONY C. RUSSELL

762 East 73rd Street, Apt. 10C
New York, NY 10021
(212) 555-7310

OBJECTIVE:

Permanent employment in a kennel leading to a managerial position

EDUCATION:

Jimmy Walker High School, New York, NY - 2000
American Boarding Kennels Association - 2000
       Completion of Stage One of the Home-Study Program

WORK EXPERIENCE:

New York City Animal Shelter - 6/99 to present
       Assist in obedience training
       Provide basic animal health care
       Bathe and groom animals
       Answer telephone inquiries

Your Pet Center - 6/98 to 9/98
       Sold pet supplies
       Cleaned cages
       Fed and watered animals

Dog Walking - 4/96 to 5/98
       Walked six animals twice a day Monday through Friday

PERSONAL:

Own and show Mitzi, a four-year-old golden retriever

REFERENCES:

Available upon request

PAULA MURRAY
308 Meredith Avenue
Missoula, MT 59812
(406) 555-3328

PROFESSIONAL OBJECTIVE
Employment as an aerobics instructor.

EDUCATIONAL BACKGROUND
2000 graduate of Missoula High School.

RELEVANT COURSE WORK
Physical Education	4 semesters
Human Relations	1 semester
Psychology	1 semester
Physiology	1 semester

ACTIVITIES
Soccer	8 years
Swimming	4 years
Basketball	2 years
Softball	2 years
Soccer Team Manager	2 years

SUMMER EMPLOYMENT
1994 - 2000
YWCA Sports Camp, Missoula, MT

Head Counselor (1998 - 2000)
Responsible for children aged 6 - 12.
Directed aerobics program.

Assistant Counselor (1994 - 1997)

REFERENCES
Available upon request.

JOHN NOWARK

217 Arthur Avenue
Omaha, NE 68103
(402) 555-5003

Career Goal:	To secure a position as an assistant greenkeeper.
Education:	**Dundee High School** Graduate, 2000

General Education
GPA 3.00/4.00 overall, 3.50/4.00 science
Science Classes:

Horticulture	2 semesters
Biology	2 semesters

Art Courses:

Ceramics	1 semester
Basic Art, Drawing	1 semester

Mathematics:

Algebra	2 semesters
Geometry	2 semesters

Experience:

Summers 1998 to 2000
Sugar Hill Nursery
453 Eureka Lane, Omaha, NE 69337

Nursery Assistant - Prepared nursery beds for planting; watered, weeded, and sprayed trees, shrubs, and plants; and filled orders.

Summers 1996 to 2000
4-H Camp
1500 Eureka Lane, Omaha, NE 69337

Counselor - Responsible for 20 children each year for one week in the month of July.

References: Available upon request.

CAROL M. LEE

1389 Stevenson Road
Denver, CO 80221
(303) 555-1275

PROFESSIONAL OBJECTIVE

A position as a journalist in a firm with opportunities to use my writing skills.

EDUCATION

Graduate of Denver City High School - 2000
English Major
GPA: 4.00/4.00
English Courses:
American Literature
Composition 1
Dreams and Myths
Composition 2
Short Story
College English
Shakespeare

EXPERIENCE

Golden Bear (school newspaper), Denver, CO

Editor (2000)
Reporter (1999)

The Coffee Pot, Denver, CO

Administrative Assistant (3/98 to present)
• Handle accounts receivable and computer input, file, and type.

Cashier (8/96 to 8/97)
• Waited on customers, answered phone, restocked shelves, and priced merchandise.

PERSONAL

Currently writing and self-publishing a collection of short stories about my family's heritage as pioneers.

REFERENCES

Furnished upon request.

NAME:	**Matt J. Pointer**
ADDRESS:	254 Vista Oaks Glendive, MT 59330
PHONE:	(406) 555-8427
OBJECTIVE:	A full-time position as an alarm technician in a firm with opportunities for advancement.
EXPERIENCE:	Assistant Alarm Technician Primary Alarm Part-time, 1997 - 2000

Assisted in the installation of various alarm systems for large companies and private residences.

EDUCATION: 2000 graduate of Vista Oaks High School
Relevant Course Work:

Keyboarding	2 semesters
Business Aide	2 semesters
Office Skills	2 semesters
Accounting	1 semester
Work Experience Ed.	3 semesters
Auto Shop	2 semesters

REFERENCES: Jack Siri
P.O. Box 578
Glendive, MT 59330
(406) 555-4308

Anne Osorio
687 Creek Drive
Lame Deer, MT 59101
(406) 555-3105

AARON C. KASAPI

276 Brooktree Ranch Rd.
Trinidad, CO 81082
(719) 555-9335

Professional Objective:	A position in architectural drafting with a construction company.
Education:	Trinidad Public High School, 1999 - 2000 Graduate 2000
	Stevenson High School, 1996 - 1999

Relevant Course Work:

Woodshop	3 years
Mechanical Drafting	1 year
Math	3 years
Architectural Drafting	2 years
CAD, Computer-Assisted Design	1 year

School Sports:

Wrestling	4 years
Soccer	2 years
Football	1 year

Special Skills:

Creating computer graphics
Working knowledge of PowerPoint
Advanced word processing applications

Affiliations:

"Out to Lunch Gang"- a band that played music
during lunchtime at high school.

Work Experience:

6/00 - 8/00	Mountain Adventures, Boulder, CO Assistant Guide
	Helped tourists manage horses, raised tents, and assisted in meal preparation.
6/99 - 8/99	Taco Bell, Trinidad, CO Crew Member
	Prepared food and cleaned restaurant.

References:

Will be made available upon request.

RITA J. FANG
304 Sierra Drive
Los Angeles, CA 90069
(310) 555-0304

POSITION DESIRED	Restaurant cashier or hostess
EDUCATION	Galileo High School Graduate, 2000
GPA 3.24/4.00

WORK
EXPERIENCE **Bayview Restaurant,** Los Angeles, CA
Title: Salad maker

Duties: Prepared salads and appetizers
Supervisor: Randy O'Neill
Dates: July to September 1999

Straw Hat Pizza, Los Angeles, CA
Title: Hostess, Cashier, Waitress, Bus-person

Duties: Greeted customers, managed customer seating, answered phone and took orders to go, operated a cash register and handled customers' money, served food, cleared tables, prepared salad bar, assisted in cooking of pizzas, and performed minimal maintenance chores
Supervisor: Marc Richards
Dates: August 1998 to May 1999

ACTIVITIES President, Galileo High School Scholarship Federation
Member, Block A Club
Member, Ski Gulls Club
Member, volleyball and basketball teams

VOLUNTEER WORK **Los Angeles County Community Blood Bank**
Title: Assistant

Duties: Comforted blood donors, served refreshments, and typed required donor forms

INTERESTS Working with people in a social atmosphere
Personal physical development program

REFERENCES Available upon request

JANICE E. KAHN
1005 Margaret Street
Willimantic, CT 06226
(203) 555-9203

Objective	Part-time position as a gardener while I attend Eastern Connecticut State University.
Schools Attended	2000 Graduate of Willimantic High School GPA 3.50/4.00
Academic Plans	To attend Eastern Connecticut State University in the fall of 2000 and major in botany.

Specialty Classes

Regional Occupational Program course of Horticulture

Human Relations	1 semester
Spanish	2 years
Biology	2 years
Keyboarding	1 semester

Community Activities	Volunteer at the Mid-County Children's Center
Hobbies and Interests	Playing the piano, gardening, crossbreeding flowers, running, and bicycling

Work Experience

Magic Farms Nursery
June to August, 1997 - 1999
354 Floral Lane, Willimantic, CT 06226

Laborer - Packed and planted sprouts, changed and lifted racks, and filled and emptied sprout bins.

Part-time housecleaning
1995 - 1997

References	Will be made available upon request.

Douglas P. Shaw
191 Cuesta Way
Boise, ID 83706
(208) 555-8599

Objective

A position in the field of graphic arts or as a photographer

Education

Capitol High School, Boise, ID
Expected graduation date: 2000

Work Experience

Precious Moments Photography, Boise, ID

Photographic Assistant
Weekends 1996 to 2000
- Set up the lights and cameras
- Mixed chemicals
- Developed film and printed photographs

Jake's Chevron Station, Boise, ID

Daytime Laborer
Summers 1998 and 1999
- Handled two cash drawers, pumped gas, and made minor repairs
- Responsible for all bookkeeping on my shifts
- Kept garage area clean

Activities

Yearbook photography editor, 2000
Yearbook head photographer, 1999
Member, varsity soccer team, 2000
Member, junior varsity soccer team, 1998, 1999

Special Skills

Photography
Web page design
Dependability
Punctuality
Making clients feel comfortable

References will be made available upon your request.

JARRON G. ADAMS

---

95 East 35th Street • Sioux City, IA 51103 • (712) 555-9025

GOAL: To work as an assistant manager in a pizza restaurant.

EDUCATION: Sioux City Central High School
                   Expected graduation date: 2000

EXPERIENCE: **MAMA'S PIZZA** - Sioux City, IA
                   Summer afternoons
                   Part-time during the school year

                   Food Preparation, 2000
                   Wash dishes, bus tables, operate cash register, and
                   make sandwiches.

                   Crew, 1998 and 1999
                   Made pizzas, bussed tables, washed dishes,
                   operated the register, and served customers.

ACTIVITIES: **RED CROSS** - Sioux City, IA
                   Volunteer Worker, 2000

INTERESTS: Skiing, waterskiing, camping, reading, hiking,
                   and being outdoors.

REFERENCES: Furnished upon request.

Jeffery R. Chuang

331 Hames Road
Belleville, IL 62221
(618) 555-5293

Objective	To become an automotive mechanic.
Education	Belleville High School - 2000

**Relevant
Course Work**

Mechanics	1 and 2
Auto Shop	2 semesters
Accounting	2 semesters

Experience

Summer 1999
Belleville Auto Body
Apprentice Bodyman

Prepared cars for painting, fixed dents, dismantled and reassembled various parts of vehicles, and washed cars.

Summers 1996 - 1998
Texaco
Station Attendant

Responsible for checking engine fluids, balancing tires, pumping gas, and related work.

Interests	Bike riding
	Skiing
	Music
Activities	Drummer for "The Fighting Fleas"
References	Available upon request.

LISA P. CHINCHIOLO

237 Hamman Drive • Chicago, IL 60606 • (312) 555-3368

OBJECTIVE:	A part-time position in a florist shop.

EXPERIENCE:

1999 - 2000   VALLEY RANCH HOMES
- Maintained plants for model homes

1995 - 1998   HOUSE AND LAWN CARE
- Did odd jobs for area houses
- Mowed and watered lawns
- Watched houses and pets
- Did some landscaping and painting

EDUCATION: Hamman High School, Chicago, IL
Expected graduation date: 2000
GPA 4.00/4.00
Plan to attend Harold Washington College, Chicago, IL.

SCHOOL ACTIVITIES: Member of the Chicago Scholarship Federation. Attended all meetings and participated in activities.
Four-year member of the Horticulture Club. Final year as President.

ADDITIONAL INFORMATION: I will graduate from Hamman High School as valedictorian with honors in science and have been named a National Merit Scholar.

REFERENCES WILL BE MADE AVAILABLE UPON YOUR REQUEST.

Joseph M. O'Connell
324 Encinal Avenue
Huntington, IN 46750
(219) 555-7419

PROFESSIONAL OBJECTIVE:
A position as a cashier/bagger with a company providing opportunities for advancement.

EXPERIENCE:

6/99 to present
ALBERTSON'S
145 Playa Boulevard
Huntington, IN 46750

My primary job was bagging; however, I also did some janitorial work.

6/98 to 9/98
PLAZA SHELL SERVICE
1872 41st Avenue
Huntington, IN 46750

My primary job was working as a cashier and completing the janitorial work.

EDUCATION:
HUNTINGTON HIGH SCHOOL - Diploma, 1999

RELEVANT COURSE WORK:

Mathematics	6 semesters
Keyboarding	1 semester
Computer Programming	1 semester
Introduction to Business	1 semester
English	6 semesters

SCHOOL ACTIVITIES:

2-year member of the soccer team
2-year member of the basketball team
3-year member of the weight-lifting club

REFERENCES:
Available on request.

Geoffery E. Pace
121 Corinne Avenue
Gary, IN 46408
(218) 555-5452

Immediate Objective: *To gain a part-time position working in a local or state park. I seek a position that will enable me to attend the local community college and obtain an Associate degree in ranger services.*

Career Objective: To become a park ranger.

Previous Work Experience:

6/00 - 8/00   Camp Carloads
                   1956 Vista Drive
                   Gary, IN 46408
                   Dishwasher

1/00 - 5/00   Gary Radio
                   92 Hanger Way
                   Gary, IN 46408
                   Phone solicitor

8/98 - 10/99   Burger King Restaurant
                   1782 Freedom Drive
                   Gary, IN 46408
                   Counter worker

Education: Gary High School, 2000
                        Gary, IN
                        GPA 2.7/4.0

School Activities: Member of the Sierra Club, 2000
                         Member of the jazz choir, 1997 - 2000
                         Member of the basketball team, 1999 - 2000

Additional Comments: I have also done yard work, including pulling weeds, splitting and stacking wood, hauling brush, and cutting trees into manageable lengths. I especially enjoy being outdoors. I learn quickly and have a well-developed work ethic.

Personal References: Available upon request.

LAURA T. MENDEZ
445 El Cerro Drive
Phoenix, AZ 85076
(602) 555-0739

OBJECTIVE
To work for an executive who needs a full-time assistant to handle routine tasks and detail work.

WORK EXPERIENCE
10-99 to present   Fantasy Cakes, Phoenix, AZ
Position: Register and counter person
Duties: Wait on customers, operate the cash register, take cake orders, and clean.

7-98 to 10-98   Mickey's One Hour Photo, Phoenix, AZ
Position: Counter person
Duties: Wait on customers, operate the cash register, develop negatives, and print pictures.

7-97 to 6-98   Pioneer Museum, Phoenix, AZ
Position: Typist
Duties: Type manuscripts, lead tours, and mow lawns.

OTHER
EXPERIENCE   President of high school student council
                     Basketball coach for junior high
                     Member of 4-H horse club

EDUCATION   Murray High School - 2000
                     GPA 3.57/4.00

RELEVANT
COURSE WORK   Keyboarding   1 year - 64 wpm
                     Accounting   1 semester
                     Computer Literacy   1 semester
                     Word Processing   1 year

REFERENCES   Will be available upon request.

MARIA G. FORTUNE

571 Vienna Drive

Pikeville, KY 41501

(606) 555-5941

OBJECTIVE:

To obtain an entry-level job in business with opportunity to enter management.

EDUCATION:

I am a recent graduate of Pikeville High School - 2000.
My grade point average was 3.85/4.00.

I have taken courses in accounting, word processing, and keyboarding (40 wpm).
I can use both IBM-compatible and Macintosh computers.

**WORK
EXPERIENCE:**

May 1998 - February 1999

	Dick Bruhns
	Pikeville, KY
Responsibilities:	Assisted customers with purchases and operated cash register.

August 1997 - May 1998

	Jacob's Drug Store
	Pikeville, KY
Responsibilities:	Wrapped customers' purchases, assisted customers, and operated cash register.

May - August 1997

	Fischer Corporation
	Pikeville, KY
Responsibilities:	Worked on inventory and did light bookkeeping.

EXTRACURRICULAR:

Member of student government, 1998, 2000
Member of yearbook staff, 1999, 2000
Member of volleyball team, 1997 - 2000

REFERENCES:

Available upon request.

ADAM E. QUAN

571 Miller Court   Slidell, LA 70460   (504) 555-1809

OBJECTIVE   To use my organizational and analytical skills in the financial industry while I continue my education toward a career as a Certified Public Accountant.

EDUCATION   Slidell High School - 2000
I plan to attend Grambling State University in Grambling, LA, and receive my Bachelor's degree in Accounting in 2004.

EMPLOYMENT

November 1999 to June 2000

Dave's Deli Restaurant, Slidell, LA.
- Managed cash receipts and cash flow of customers' activity as a cashier
- Maintained good customer relations through hosting.
- Provided clean work areas by bussing workstations.

June 1999 to September 1999

The Lodge, Slidell, LA.
- Handled the opening and closing procedures of both the restaurant and store facility.
- Responsible for customer service, which included cashiering, bussing workstations, and hosting.

November 1998 to June 1998

Dave's Deli Restaurant, Slidell, LA.
- Trained as a cashier; learned how to manage cash transactions.
- Handled payment transactions for customers.
- Trained in the importance of customer relations through hosting.

REFERENCES AVAILABLE UPON REQUEST.

PABLO A. RAMIREZ

261 Baltusrol Way
Baton Rouge, LA 70803
(504) 555-5069

Job Goal	A permanent part-time position as a salesperson and cashier.
Education	Central High School - 1999
	143 Central Street, Baton Rouge, LA 70803
	Course work for a business major:
	Accounting
	Economics
	Psychology
School Activities	Four-year member of football team
	Four-year member of SADD (Students Against Drunk Driving)
	Three-year member of the Business Club: President my final year.
Work Experience	**Blockbuster Video**
	435 Desilva Street
	Baton Rouge, LA 70803
	Duties: sales and cashier
	Sidney's Food Store
	200 Desilva Street
	Baton Rouge, LA 70803
	Duties: sales, cashier, and telephone

Personal Statement

I am a warm, sincere person who is eager to learn and willing to work hard.

References	Available Upon Request

Name	**JAMES C. RICHARDS**
Address	1740 Webster Woods Drive
	Lake Charles, LA 70609 (318) 555-2347
Career Objective	A position in business management in which I can use my skills in the areas of strategic management, business research, and information management.
Education	Lake Charles High School Graduate, 1999
	GPA 3.4/4.0
Relevant Courses	Advanced Mathematics
	AP Computer Science
	Business I, II
	Accounting

Work History

Hughes Union 76
Lake Charles, LA
April 1999 to September 1999

Station Attendant
Duties: Helped customers at the full-service island and at the self-service island. Did minor mechanical repairs: radiator hoses, tires, batteries, and belts. This job indicates my ability to work with demanding and frustrated customers in pressure situations.

Tribune (newspaper)
Lake Charles, LA
June 1998 to September 1998

Paper Inserter
Duties: Began work at 12:00 A.M. and prepared newspapers for delivery. The job was usually completed in four hours. This job indicates my ability to work diligently regardless of time of day.

References available upon request.

GEORGIA R. HOLIDAY
576 Mesquite Drive
Waterville, ME 04901
(207) 555-8458

OBJECTIVE

To find a job that calls for learning and creativity and offers advancement in a friendly, people-oriented atmosphere.

EDUCATION

1999 Graduate of Waterville High School in Waterville, ME
Grade Point Average 3.6/4.0

Areas of Concentration:

English	Four years
Mathematics	Four years
Business education	Two years

WORK EXPERIENCE

The King's Service
Cleaning Service
1998 to 1999

Clerical Worker: Typed up work orders, filed, and answered business telephone.

The Perfect Place
Clothing Store
Summer 1998

Sales Clerk: Sold clothing during sidewalk sales.

Floral Furnishings
Wholesale Florist Supply
Summer 1997

Clerical Worker: Wrote orders, did stock control, filed business papers, and answered business telephone.

REFERENCES AVAILABLE UPON REQUEST

FRANCINE P. SMITH

---

786 Quartz Street
Bangor, ME 04401
(207) 555-8692

Occupational Goal:	I would like to become a dietician. Presently, I am seeking a part-time job that will allow me to attend school in order to prepare for my chosen field.
Education:	High School: Bangor High School Degree: High school diploma, 2000 Grade average: A-/B+
Special Skills:	I learn rapidly and work well with other people. I am skilled in word processing and using the Internet.
Hobbies:	Exercising Skiing Playing the guitar
Activities:	Member of the Bangor High School Key Club and American Field Service during my junior year. Member of the Bangor High School Concert and Marching Band during my freshman and sophomore years.

Work Experience:

6/00 - 9/00	Child-care provider for fifteen hours a week.
9/99 - 5/00	Housecleaner for three to four hours per week.
6/98 - 8/99	Baby-sitter for four to five hours a week.
References:	Available upon request.

NICOLA E. RHODES
938 Indiana Avenue
Augusta, ME 04330
(207) 555-5809

OBJECTIVE

To obtain a part-time position with a firm whose focus is public relations. The position should lead to a full-time position after graduation from college.

EDUCATION

2000 Student at Farmington University
Business and French major

1999 Graduate of Augusta High School
GPA 3.8/4.0

SPECIAL ABILITIES AND STUDIES

I have taken advanced courses in mathematics, French, English literature, business, science, and computer technology and programming.

I speak fluent French.

I am experienced with a computerized cash register.

PREVIOUS EMPLOYMENT
Burger King Restaurant
200 Main Street, Augusta, ME
September 1999 to January 2000

Duties: Cashier (computerized)
                 Food preparation
                 Dishwasher

REFERENCES AVAILABLE UPON REQUEST

ANGELA T. SANCHEZ

301 Coates Way
Alpena, MI 49707
(517) 555-8104

Objective: Part-time position in communications that would use my past experiences while enabling me to continue my studies at Andrews University in Berrien Springs, MI. Position should include promotional possibilities.

Education: **Alpena High School, 1999**
I will attend Andrews University beginning in the fall of 2000.
I plan to receive my Bachelor's degree in Communications in 2004.

Work Experience:

June 1999 to
Present

Customer Relations/Secretary
Jim's Audio Video Service Co.
Responsibilities: helping customers, filing, answering phones, ordering parts, and recording accounts payable and accounts receivable.

August 1998

Researcher
County Supervisors' Campaign Committee
Responsibilities: performing microfilm research.

June 1997 to
August 1997

Office Assistant
Alpena Board of Realtors
Responsibilities: putting together and mailing newsletters, filing, and typing.

Other Experience:

Member of varsity tennis and softball teams, 1998 - 1999.
Member of yearbook staff - reporter and layout designer, 1998 - 1999.
Member of Michigan Scholarship Association, 1998 - 1999.
Proficient in Spanish.

References: Available upon request.

CHRISTIANNA M. NELSON

900 Bear Valley Drive   Escanaba, MI 49829   (906) 555-2380

IMMEDIATE OBJECTIVE

To obtain a position as a physical therapist aide enabling me to work with physically disabled individuals while I attend college. I would prefer employment with a company that would be able to place me in a permanent physical therapist position once I have graduated from college.

LONG-TERM OBJECTIVE

To become a physical therapist.

EDUCATION

Escanaba High School in Escanaba, MI - 1999
GPA 3.9/4.0

My educational plans are to attend Calvin College in Grand Rapids, MI. I plan to major in education of the physically handicapped.

ACADEMIC ACTIVITIES

I was a member of the high school Interact Club (a community service organization) for four years. I was president of the club my senior year.

EMPLOYMENT HISTORY

Summers 1998, 1999   BAY DE NOC CAMP, Madison, WI

Camp Counselor for developmentally disabled teenagers and adults.

Academic years 1997, 1998, 1999
                          ESCANABA HIGH SCHOOL, Escanaba, MI

Volunteer Aide to Special Education teacher.

REFERENCES AVAILABLE UPON REQUEST.

MARTHA BIGELOW

Current Address:
468 East 25th Street
Charlottesville, VA 22906
(804) 555-8723
mbigelow@aol.com

Permanent Address:
2005 Bristol Avenue
Richmond, VA 23284
(804) 555-9737

OBJECTIVE

An entry-level systems analyst position for a manufacturing or software firm. Desire to progress to position providing systems management to client companies. Seek an opportunity to use my leadership and communication skills.

EDUCATION

UNIVERSITY OF VIRGINIA, Charlottesville, VA
Bachelor of Science: May 2000, Computer Information Systems
Major GPA: 3.5

STUDENT EXCHANGE PROGRAM, Florence, Italy - Summer 1997

RELEVANT EXPERIENCE

5/99 - 8/99

AT&T GLOBAL INFORMATION SOLUTIONS, Milan, Italy
Intern, Financial Planning and Inventory Accounting Departments:
Analyzed improvements in time, money, and paperwork that would result from the use of the new purchasing system. Performed cost analysis of new PC units for future pricing. Wrote macros in Excel and Word to make exporting of files easier in each file format. Translated reports, letters, and phone calls from Italian to English and vice versa.

8/98 - 10/99

AT&T, Charlottesville, VA
Communications Representative:
Marketed the AT&T MasterCard, phone card, and phone company to students.

5/98 - 8/98

RICHMOND HILLS TENNIS CLUB, Richmond, VA
Tennis Instructor: Developed and managed a tennis program for pupils of different ages and skill levels at a community facility. Marketed the program aggressively. Hired four tennis instructors because of program's growth.

ACTIVITIES

DELTA SIGMA PI BUSINESS FRATERNITY
Offices Held: Vice President for chapter operations, Secretary, Sergeant-at-Arms
Major Accomplishment: Launched first Mini Ironman Competition for American Cancer Society and raised more than $10,000.

UNIVERSITY OF VIRGINIA STUDENT GOVERNMENT
Governor: Elected to represent 500 students in Stern Hall.

ALPHA PHI SORORITY
Panhellenic Council Delegate: Served as a sorority liaison and voting representative.

UNIVERSITY OF VIRGINIA RECRUITING REPRESENTATIVE
Tour Guide: Led campus and dormitory tours for prospective university students.

PERSONAL INFORMATION

Skilled in Windows, C/C++, Lotus, Excel, Word, and COBOL MVS. Traveled extensively in Europe. Conversational Italian. Member of the Richmond High School State Champion Tennis Team. Enjoy tennis, jogging, and outdoor activities.

REFERENCES

Available on request.

Joshua K. Peck
301 Coates Drive
International Falls, MN 56649
(218) 555-2452

Objective: To become an actor in a community theater.

Acting Experience: Member of the Drama Club for four years.
                        Major role in *The People vs Maxine Loe*, 1999.
                        Major role in *Our Town*, 1998.
                        Major role in *Arsenic and Old Lace*, 1997.

Work Experience:

June 1999 to Present **McDonald's Restaurant**
                      International Falls, MN

Responsibilities: operate cash register, improve and maintain the site and lobby, make fries, cook the food, and close the restaurant at night.

June 1998   **Taco Bell Restaurant**
to August 1998   International Falls, MN

Responsibilities: operated electronic cash register, prepared and packaged the food, and cleaned and maintained restaurant.

Personal: Competed in track-and-field for six years.
                        I was a multi-event winner and team captain
                        my senior year.

                        Member of the football team for two years: 1998, 1999.

                        Fluent in written and conversational French.

Education: Graduated from International Falls High School in 1999.
                        Drama Society award winner, 1999.

Plan to attend St. Cloud State University in St. Cloud, MN, in 2000. I will major in Speech/Communication/Theater Education and will graduate in 2004.

References: Available upon request.

HANK MADRUGA

243 Shoreview Way
Minneapolis, MN 55454
(612) 555-7080

OBJECTIVE
To become a sales clerk in a major department store.

WORK EXPERIENCE
December 1999 - present:

Pete's Deli-Cafe
Minneapolis, MN
> *General helper: responsible for operating cash register, taking food orders, doing dishes, making decisions concerning supplies, catering, stocking supplies, dealing with the public, and preparing some food.*

Prior to December 1999:

Miscellaneous Jobs
> *Housecleaned, baby-sat, gardened, and cashiered at a bookstore.*

OTHER EXPERIENCE
- Member, Lakeside High School newspaper staff
- Member, Lakeside High School ski club
- Member, Lakeside High School baseball team
- Member, Lakeside High School swim team
- Member, Lakeside High School track-and-field team
- Member, Lakeside High School cross-country team

EDUCATION
Lakeside High School, Minneapolis, MN, 1999
GPA 2.8/4.0

REFERENCES
Will be made available upon your request.

JOSEFINA Y. ALONZO

236 Quail Run
Denver, CO 80222
(303) 555-1498

OBJECTIVE:

To become a professional ski instructor.

WORK EXPERIENCE:

| | Ski Lift Operator, Ski Instructor |
| Winters, 1998, 1999, 2000 | Hesperus Ski Area, Durango, CO |

Worked lifts, reported problems, taught children and adults how to ski.

| | Busboy, Food Preparer |
| June 1999 to August 1999 | The Wild Side Cafe, Durango, CO |

Bussed tables, washed dishes, and prepared food for the next day.

OTHER EXPERIENCE:

Member of Durango Ski Rescue Team, 2000
Member of high school ski team, 1997 - 2000
Member of Denver Youth Group, 1998

EDUCATION:

2000 Graduate of Roosevelt High School
Denver, CO

REFERENCES:

References will be furnished upon request.

Frank P. Reyes

988 El Sereno Court
Stratham, NH 03885
(603) 555-1798

OBJECTIVE

To work as a part-time chef while I attend classes at New Hampshire Culinary Academy in Stratham, NH. The job should include the possibility of promotion and a full-time position after I graduate from the Academy.

EDUCATION

Stratham High School, Stratham, NH
General Studies Diploma, 2000
GPA 2.9/4.0
Relevant Course Work:

Restaurant - internship	two semesters
Nutrition	one semester
Food Chemistry	two semesters
English	four years
French	four years

WORK EXPERIENCE

June 1999 to August 1999
Food Service Worker
Rudolph's Restaurant
267 Lahai Roi Street, Stratham, NH 03885

Responsibilities: Preparing food for the next day, operating the cash register, and grill chef.

June 1998 to August 1998
Food Service Worker
Dairy Queen
489 Cross Street, Stratham, NH 03885

Responsibilities: Managing cash flow, acting as night manager occasionally, operating the cash register, cooking, and preparing food.

REFERENCES WILL BE MADE AVAILABLE UPON YOUR REQUEST.

Elly G. Minch

245 Chaparral Drive
Chester, NH 03036
(603) 555-1364

Objective:

To secure a part-time job as a cashier that will enable me to attend classes and earn money to pay for my college education.

Education:

Chester High School - 1999
764 Chaparral Drive
Chester, NH 03036
GPA 3.5/4.0

I will be attending Notre Dame College, Manchester, NH, in the fall of 1999. I plan to major in psychology.

School Activities and Course Work:

Business Education - 2 semesters

Keyboarding and Word Processing - 2 years. Helped teach classmates computer skills.

Varsity swim team member for 3 years - school's top swimmer

Work Experience:

June to August 1999   Cashier (part-time)
Baskin Robbins - ice cream parlor
Opened store on weekends and handled some bookkeeping.

June to August 1998   Cashier (part-time)
Candy's Kitchen - restaurant

References:

Available upon request.

EMANUEL R. MARTINEZ

234 Kingsbury Drive, Auburn, NY 13021
(315) 555-6757

Objective: To secure part-time employment in the field of business management while I continue my education.

Education: Auburn High School - 1999
GPA - 3.8/4.0

In the fall, I will attend Canisius College in Buffalo, NY. I plan to major in business administration and management. I will graduate in 2003.

Activities:
- Volunteer food server at Friday's Food Center for the homeless twice a month.

- Four-year member of the Auburn High School speech group, Junior Statesmen of America.

- Four-year member of the Auburn High School Varsity Football Team, team captain senior year.

Work Experience: June to August, 1997, 1998, 1999
Salesman, Delivery Driver, Cashier
The One Stop Shop, Auburn, NY
I started in merchandising, became a cashier, and was promoted to delivery driver.

Special Skills: Built and sold furniture; designed and constructed promotional signs and merchandise displays; learned the workings of shipping and receiving departments; trained personnel for all jobs mentioned above.

General: I am a creative worker who is artistically inclined. I can do challenging jobs both thoroughly and efficiently. I am communicative with the public as well as with my fellow employees. I am capable of sticking with a job as is shown by my work experience.

References: Will be available when requested.

KIMBERLY C. BAKER
456 Baltusrol Way
Tarboro, NC 27886
(919) 555-0922

OBJECTIVE   A part-time job as a receptionist for a company that offers the possibility of promotion into business management.

EDUCATION   1999 Tarboro High School
GPA 3.20/4.00

My educational plans are to attend Edgecombe Community College in Tarboro, NC, full-time for the next 2 years. I will transfer to East Carolina University in Greenville, NC, to obtain my bachelor's degree in business administration and management.

EXPERIENCE   **RECEPTIONIST**
Leon T. Beacom, CPA
Tarboro, NC
Summers 1998 and 1999

Responsibilities: Answering phones, filing papers, and making client appointments.

SCOREKEEPER
Tarboro Youth Basketball Association
Tarboro, NC
November to February, 1997, 1998, and 1999

Responsibilities: Writing score sheets, recording the score, and reporting score results to the newspaper.

**OTHER
EXPERIENCE**
- Member of Student Government at Tarboro High for 3 years. Associated Student Body President senior year.
- Member of the Tarboro High varsity basketball team for 3 years. Played junior varsity basketball for 1 year.
- Member of the Tarboro High varsity softball team for 3 years.
- Member of Tarboro High varsity track for 1 year.
- Member of Tarboro High SADD (Students Against Drunk Driving) club.
- Worked at the Special Olympics for 2 years.

REFERENCES UPON REQUEST

Tracey Warrick
467 Altivo Drive
Yellow Springs, OH 45387
(513) 555-1875
twarrick@aol.com

Objective:
To serve as a part-time travel agent in a firm that provides the possibility of advancement and a full-time position once I have graduated from college.

Work Experience: **June 2000 to present**
Word Processor, Data Entry
The Book Worm, Yellow Springs, OH
Responsibilities: Answering correspondence, entering data including account receivables, and mailing information.

Prior to June 2000
Miscellaneous jobs such as baby-sitting, house-sitting, and housecleaning.

Other Experience:
• Competitive Swimming: My participation with the Yellow Springs High School swim team and the Aqua Devils swim team has increased my ability to handle competition and stress.

• Leadership: I was in charge of the operation of the Yellow Springs High School Blood Bank for two years.

• Travel: I am experienced in many different kinds of travel including camping, backpacking, and canoeing.

Education: 2000 Graduate of Yellow Springs High School
GPA 2.6/4.0

• I am currently enrolled in two night courses focused on the travel agency business: Regional Occupational Program and a computer course on the Apollo series working with the computerized OAG.

• My educational plans are to major in communications and to graduate from Antioch College in Yellow Springs, OH in 2004.

References available upon request.

Matt M. LeRoy

College Address: Home Address:
45 East Campus Drive   33 Pleasant Drive
Ames, IA 50011   Storm Lake, IA 50588
(515) 555-9600   (712) 555-9232

Objective: To obtain an entry-level position that uses my computer and business
                   skills and challenges me to grow professionally.

Education: Iowa State University of Science and Technology, Ames, Iowa
                   Major: Applied Computer Science   Minor: Business Administration
                   Expected date of graduation: May 2001

                   Relevant Course Work:
                   Computer Application and Design, External Data Structures, Data Struc-
                   tures, Introduction to Systems Development, Database Processing, Sys-
                   tem Development Tools and Issues

**Work
Experience:**   Computer Programmer/Analyst Internship, Caterpillar, Inc.,
                   Des Moines, IA
5/00 - 8/00   • Maintaining/testing on-line programs
                   • Designing/testing batch programs using COBOL MVS

9/99 - 3/00   Maintenance Worker, Central Iowa Trucking, Storm Lake, IA
                   • Keeping shop area in order, running errands
                   • Computer data entry

1/98 - 8/99   Farm Worker, Peterson Farms, Storm Lake, IA
                   • Year-round operation and maintenance of farm machinery

Skills: Able to use computers to solve problems. Fluent in COBOL MVS,
                   C/C++, and Visual Basic. Experience with WordPerfect,
                   Microsoft Office 2000

**Honors and
Scholarships:**   Iowa State University of Science and Technology
                   • Governor's Scholar, 1997
                   • Freshman Entrance Writing Examination - winner
                   Iowa State Scholar, 1997
                   Valedictorian, Storm Lake High School

Activities: Varsity member of the university football and wrestling teams
                   for 4 years

References: Available upon request

CAROL M. LOOMIS

---

85 Peace Drive
Portland, OR 97219
(503) 555-0186

OBJECTIVE: A part-time position as a children's dance instructor that will enable me to attend college classes while teaching.

EDUCATION: June 2000 Graduate of Lakeside High School Portland, OR
GPA 3.00/4.00

In Fall 2000, I will attend Lewis and Clark College in Portland, OR. I will graduate in 2004 with a Bachelor's degree in Dramatic Arts.

WORK EXPERIENCE: Assistant Dance Instructor
The Dance Studio, Portland, OR

Responsibilities: teaching tap and jazz to school-aged children.
Summers 1998, 1999

SPECIAL ACTIVITIES: Two-year member of Jazz Dancers group in high school.
Four years jazzercize.
Six years tap and ballet lessons.

REFERENCES: Cathy Delude, dance instructor,
The Dance Studio
(503) 555-1154

Norman Haney, family friend
(503) 555-7600

Norman L. Potter
4322 Clares Street
Butler, PA 16003
(412) 555-6897

OBJECTIVE

To obtain a part-time position with an architectural firm that will enable me to gain experience in the field of architecture. The position should provide the possibility for advancement with the completion of my scholastic studies.

EDUCATION

Butler High School, Butler, PA, 1999
Graduated in the top 20 percent of the class
GPA: 3.2/4.0
Next year, I will attend Butler County Community College where I plan to major in drafting.

WORK EXPERIENCE

Food Service Worker   June 1999 to August 1999

McDonald's Restaurant, Butler, PA
Responsible for taking and preparing food orders, operating the cash register, preparing food, cleaning lobby and food area, and stocking supplies.

General Worker   Prior to June 1999

Miscellaneous Jobs
Performed baby-sitting and gardening tasks.

OTHER EXPERIENCE

Completion of Drafting 1 and 2 courses in high school
Proficient in computer-assisted design

References available upon request.

MORGAN A. WRIGHT

896 Mesa Drive
Columbia, SC 29208
(803) 555-4079

OBJECTIVE	To become a limousine driver.
WORK EXPERIENCE	**Columbia Pizza Company, Columbia, SC**
	Dough Roller

Responsibilities:
        Providing a clean work area
        Flouring the table
        Rolling and cutting the dough
        Mixing the dough batch for the following day

The Supreme Pizza, Columbia, SC

Busboy

Responsibilities:
        Completing "prep list"
        Collecting dishes
        Putting dishes away
        Cleaning restaurant and closing up

OTHER EXPERIENCE	Hold South Carolina chauffeur's license
	Member of DeYoung High School Jazz Band
EDUCATION	Recent graduate of DeYoung High School
	Columbia, SC
	GPA: 2.5/4.0

Full references will be provided on request.

AMY J. FENNELL

445 Polo Drive
Portland, OR 97201
(503) 555-1967

OBJECTIVE

To be a fashion designer

EDUCATION

High School: Upland High School
Degree: High school diploma - 1999
Grade Average: B
In the fall of 2000, I will attend Bassist College
in Portland, OR, where I plan to receive an
Associate degree in fashion design.

ACTIVITIES

My junior year I helped start a new group at
Upland High School called SADD (Students
Against Drunk Driving). I was the group's
treasurer my senior year.

I was a member of Junior Statesmen of
America (JSA) my junior and senior years.

My sophomore and junior years, I kept
statistics for the junior varsity basketball team.

During my freshman year, I kept statistics for
the freshman basketball team.

WORK EXPERIENCE

Miscellaneous jobs such as lawn mowing
and baby-sitting.

References will be provided upon your request.

Johnny K. Litchfield

452 Baja Sol Drive
Sioux Falls, SD 57197
(605) 555-9506

Objective:	A permanent position as a carpenter.
Work Experience:	Jack's Pizza Sioux Falls, SD Dishwasher Period of Service: 4 months
Education:	1999 Graduate of Sioux Falls High School Grade Average B- Relevant Courses: Construction I, II Mechanical Drawing

Special Skills:

Woodworking	Three years as a hobby
Landscaping	One year in home garden
Bassist	Currently performing in a band

References:

Jack Core	Richard Crivello
Owner, Jack's Pizza	Family Friend
(605) 555-0793	(605) 555-3702

DEBBIE R. NEWELL
2986 Middle Avenue
Rapid City, SC 57701
(605) 555-1307

OBJECTIVE: Full-time employment as a secretary while
                        I attend night classes.

PARTICULARS: • Typing - 75 wpm
                        • WordPerfect, Word
                        • Lotus, PowerPoint, Quicken

EDUCATION: **Rapid City High School,** Rapid City, SC
                        Degree: 2000 General Studies

                        I will attend Western Dakota Vocational Technical
                        Institute for 2 years beginning in the fall of 2000.

WORK EXPERIENCE: **Kmart**
                        Clerk - women's clothing department
                        Cash Register Operator
                        9/98 to present
                        Full-time during the summer
                        Part-time during the academic year

EXTRACURRICULAR: • Member of the high school choir and jazz choir.
                        • Participated in Girl Scout activities for 3 years.
                        • Served as a camp counselor for Brownies
                          and Pixies at the City Park.

REFERENCES: Available upon your request.

ANGELA R. CHACON

564 Meadowview Court
Castleton, VT 05735
(802) 555-8102

OBJECTIVE

To work in the art/graphic design department of an advertising agency.

WORK EXPERIENCE

Customer Relations/Secretary
Designs Unlimited
Castleton, VT
June to August 2000

Office Assistant
Penn Ad Agency
Castleton, VT
June to August 1999

Baby-sitting
Prior to June 1999

OTHER EXPERIENCE

Member of yearbook staff, 1999 - 2000
Member of Castleton Scholarship Federation, 1999 - 2000
Member of varsity tennis and softball teams, 1998 - 2000
Fluent in Spanish

EDUCATION

I graduated from Castleton High School in June 2000. My educational plans are to attend Castleton State College in Castleton, VT, where I will major in drawing and fine arts.

REFERENCES

Will be provided upon your request.

NAME: Carla Grant

ADDRESS: 2976 Lucky Lane
                   Cleveland, TN 37320

TELEPHONE: (615) 555-1745

OBJECTIVE: Full-time position in a clothing store as a sales clerk.

EDUCATION: Knoxville High School, 2000
                   Knoxville, TN
                   GPA 3.0/4.0

                   My educational plans are to attend Cleveland State Community
                   College part-time. I will major in marketing and sales.

EXPERIENCE: JCPenney
                   May 2000 to present
                     Cash register operator

                   The Emporium
                   January 1998 to November 1999
                     Sales clerk

EXTRACURRICULAR:
                   • Junior Achievement, 1999, 2000
                   • Member of Zenith Group (a public speaking club), 2000
                   • Sophomore Magazine Sales - Class Coordinator, 1998

QUALIFICATIONS:
                   I am a committed, hardworking, and punctual employee who
                   interacts skillfully with customers.

REFERENCES: Kay Dietze, Junior Achievement Sponsor (615) 555-2778
                   Linda Nealis, JCPenney (615) 555-4410

Kyle J. Ahn

589 Bavington Drive
Nashville, TN 37209
(615) 555-4589

Objective
Full-time employment in the field of business management.

Work Experience
Kroger
Nashville, TN
Position: Courtesy Clerk
Responsibilities: Bagging groceries, serving customers, and maintaining site.
June to August 2000

The Fish Bowl Pet Center
Nashville, TN
Position: Assistant Manager
Responsibilities: Selling, maintaining shop, ordering supplies, closing out register, opening and closing the store.
June to August 1999

Special Skills
Proficient with Word and Excel
Keyboarding - 60 wpm
Able to work well with customers and coworkers

Education
Graduate of Memorial High School - 2000
GPA: 2.75/4.00
Four-year member of boys' volleyball team
Four-year member of Business Club
My future educational goals are to attend Nashville State Technical Institute part-time, majoring in business. I plan to work full-time while attending college.

References
Peter Lane, Owner, The Fish Bowl, (615) 555-0765
Donna Staley, neighbor, (615) 555-1365
Ron Nix, family friend, (615) 555-5502

RENALDO G. MADRIGAL

290 Hampshire Road
Provo, UT 84602
(901) 555-1834

Objective   Part-time managerial position with a small business.

Work Experience

June 2000 to August 2000	**Arco Station** Provo, UT Station Attendant Responsibilities: Operating cash register, light stocking, and cleaning.
March 2000 to June 2000	**The Water Hole** Provo, UT Swim School Maintenance Responsibilities: Add chlorine as necessary. Clean and vacuum pool.
Prior to March 2000	**Woodland Timber** Wood Cutter and Splitter Provo, UT Responsibilities: Cut, split, and hauled wood for personal use and profit.

Other Experience
- Experienced in fiberglass repair.
- Member of Utah Scholarship Federation - 4 years.
- Member of varsity soccer team - 2 years. Team captain senior year.
- Member of junior varsity soccer team. Received valuable player award - 1998.
- Fluent in Spanish.
- Three-year member of Big Brother, Big Sister program.

Education

2000 Graduate of Provo High School
- GPA 3.1/4.0
- My educational plans are to attend Brigham Young University in Provo, UT. My degree objective is to obtain a B.A. in business.

References will be provided upon your request.

Dale Crivello

275 Huntington Drive
Middlebury, VT 05753
(802) 555-4294

Objective: Part-time position as a chef or assistant chef providing the
opportunity of advancement upon my graduation from college.

Education: Middlebury High School
- Expected graduation date: 2000
- GPA: 3.5/4.0
- Relevant course work:
    Mathematics through Geometry
    Home Economics 1 and 2
    Nutrition
    2 years of French
- I will attend New England Culinary Institute in Montpelier, VT,
  in the fall. I will major in food production, management,
  and services.

Work Experience:

2/99 - 8/99   **Denny's Restaurant**
                     I was the preparation cook.

6/98 - 8/98   **Swensen's Ice Cream Factory**
                     I dipped cones and decorated various ice-cream products.

Other Experience:

- Varsity football team, 4 years, MVP senior year
- Soccer league, 4 years
- Ski club, 4 years

References: Available on request.

ROGER NEWTON 765 Murphy's Lane • Arlington, VA 22207 • (703) 555-3099

OBJECTIVE: To become a full-time auto mechanic.

EDUCATION: 2000 Graduate of Arlington High School
GPA 2.5/4.0
Relevant course work:

• Auto shop	2 years
• Auto shop student supervisor	1 year
• Business math	1 year

EXPERIENCE:

6/99 to present   ARLINGTON SHELL, Arlington, VA
Station Attendant
Responsible for operating the cash register, assisting customers, checking oil, washing windows, checking tire pressure, and fixing flat tires.

Prior to 6/99   ODD JOBS
Gardening, dog walking, catering, cleanup work, and car repair.

ACTIVITIES: 4-year member high school morning weight-lifting club
2-year member high school spirit club
1-year member high school business club

INTERESTS: Customizing vans
Attending NASCAR races
Racing motorcycles

REFERENCES PROVIDED ON REQUEST

LINDA JEAN COLLINS
5071 Illinois Road
Santa Fe, NM 87504
(505) 555-5452

EDUCATION

9/97 - present
College of Santa Fe, anticipate Bachelor's degree in Theological Studies (with Honors), June 2001. Current GPA: 3.7/4.0

EXPERIENCE

7/00 - 9/00
Counselor, Hill Top Lodge, Albuquerque, NM. Led Bible studies, taught athletics and lifestyle seminars for high school students.

10/99 - 12/99
Security Agent, Santa Fe College Bookstore. Handled surveillance activities and arrest of violators. Also, ensured store safety and transported funds.

6/96 - 9/98
Services Department, Osee, Ling (law firm), Santa Fe, NM. Dealt with court filings, couriers, mail, and distribution. Acted as receptionist.

1997 - present
Tutor, Santa Fe College Christian Ministries Tutoring Program. Volunteer on a weekly basis with an underprivileged child.

1996 - present
Youth Fellowship, Santa Fe Presbyterian Church. Lead small group Bible studies, coordinate welcoming and hospitality committees, participate in prayer groups, serve at soup kitchens and children's camps.

ADDITIONAL INFORMATION

- Participated with my high school youth group on several work projects at churches and orphanages in Mexico.

- Treasurer, Chi Omega House, Santa Fe College.

- Social Chairman, Freshman Orientation Committee, Santa Fe College.

References available upon request.

JASMINE K. LAKE

Present Address: Permanent Address:
P.O. Box 04834   5606 Castle Avenue
Baltimore, MD 21218   Langston, OK 73050
(301) 555-0523   (405) 555-3247

OBJECTIVE: To obtain a position in the entering class of a top medical school
                        and pursue a career in research-oriented medicine.

EDUCATION: Johns Hopkins University, Baltimore, MD
                        Bachelor of Science, Biology, with honors, June 2000
                        Overall GPA: 3.83   Science GPA: 3.89

RESEARCH EXPERIENCE:

Research Investigator, Molecular Endocrinology Lab, Johns Hopkins Medical
Center (1998 - 2000). Studied the relationship between stem cell factor protein
and the Sertoli cell only and germ cell arrest male infertility syndromes.
Assisted on projects studying inhibin protein transcription and translation rates.
Helped plan, coordinate, and carry out research. Learned and used techniques
such as Southern blots, cell cultures, reverse transcriptase polymerase chain
reactions, and single-stranded conformational polymorphism. Prepared data
and reports for publication.

Research and Clinical Assistant, Department of Neurology, Baltimore
Veteran's Administration Outpatient Clinic (1997). Studied neuromuscular
diseases and the ability of human muscle to survive different methods of
storage. Learned a variety of pathology techniques. Assisted with neurological
examinations such as EEGs.

OTHER WORK EXPERIENCE:

Tutor, Johns Hopkins University, Baltimore, MD (1997 - 1998).
Assisted other students with English, mathematics, physics, and biology.

ADDITIONAL INFORMATION:

- *Member,* Student Radio Board of Directors,
  Johns Hopkins University.
- *Volunteer,* "Tiny Tots" Nursery School, Johns Hopkins Special
  Olympics, Drunk Driving Prevention Program,
  and Free Peer Tutoring.
- *Member,* Committee on Housing and Residential Education,
  Johns Hopkins University.

REFERENCES: Available upon your request.

Stephanie Brown

Present Address:
P.O. Box 5041
Baton Rouge, LA 70802
(504) 555-2398

Permanent Address:
7893 Virginian Lane
Ashland, KY 41101
(606) 555-1365

Education:
Grantham College of Engineering - 9/97 to present
Expected to graduate in 6/01 with Bachelor's degree in Computer Engineering.

Experience:

Summer Intern   6/00 - 9/00
Tandem Computers, Slidell, LA
- Worked with Mechanical Design Group
- Managed the receiving and shipping of prototype parts
- Assembled and evaluated prototype parts and systems
- Redesigned problem parts
- Edited and prepared graphic design for departmental handbook

Part-Time Intern   4/99 - 9/99
Pillar Corporation, Ashland, KY
- Learned the inside workings of a small design consulting firm
- Researched current products to focus design of new concepts
- Designed ideas for new dinnerware sets

Summer Intern   6/98 - 9/98
Praxis Design Inc., Ashland, KY
- Used visual editors to alter program resources
- Edited program code
- Designed program icons and screens

Current Activities:
Member, Kappa Kappa Gamma Sorority

Hobbies:
Skiing, biking, camping, hiking, running, and playing the violin

References:
Available upon request

Sample Cover Letters

2005 Bristol Avenue
Richmond, VA 23284
(804) 555-9737
m.bigelow@aol.com

March 5, 2000

William Benedict
Federated Phone Company
87 Commercial Street
Santa Clara, CA 95054

Dear Mr. Benedict:

Dick Poon of AT&T referred me to you because of your firm's need for an analyst to evaluate costs and pricing of several of your new communications products. I would be very interested in discussing this position with you.

I will be graduating from the University of Virginia in May 2000. My studies at the university have prepared me well to contribute to your organization. My quantitative skills have been sharpened by course work in calculus and statistics.

At AT&T, I received firsthand exposure to the pricing of new PC units. I believe that the tools I acquired there could effectively be translated to analyzing your company's products.

My resume is enclosed for your review. I will call you on Friday to set up an appointment to talk about how I might be useful to Federated Phone Company. I look forward to meeting with you.

Sincerely,

Martha Bigelow

Enclosure

P.O. Box 5041
Baton Rouge, LA 70802
September 20, 2001

Knute Jameson
Entergy
Human Resources Department
225 Baronne St.
New Orleans, LA 70112

Dear Mr. Jameson:

This letter is in response to your advertisement in the *New Orleans Picayune* on September 18, 2001, for a design consultant.

Currently, I am pursuing my bachelor's degree in computer engineering at Grantham College of Engineering. I plan to graduate in December 2001. I have taken several courses in computer programming as part of my major and feel confident of my ability to learn and master any design program.

Through my summer employment, I have gained practical experience in design concepts using computer programming. I believe that my work experience will allow me to make an immediate and valuable contribution to Entergy.

As requested, I am enclosing my resume for your review. I would appreciate the opportunity to discuss my qualifications and abilities in more depth at an interview.

Sincerely yours,

Stephanie Brown
(504) 555-2398

enclosure

48 Hickory Drive
Houston, TX 77002
(713) 555-4968

May 23, 2000

Joseph Lanz
Lanz and Associates at Law
2100 Main Street
Houston, TX 77002

Dear Mr. Lanz:

Thank you for talking with me on May 21, 2000, about the secretarial position at your law office. Our conversation made me very interested in becoming a member of your staff. With my past work experience and extensive course work in accounting, mathematics, and typing (56 wpm), I feel that I could be a valuable employee at Lanz and Associates at Law.

This June, I will graduate from Victoria High School. Should I be hired by your law firm, I would be available to work full-time from the 12th of June to the 24th of August. From August 24th on, I would be able to work a maximum of five hours each day. My work hours would be reduced because I will be attending college.

Thank you for your time. I look forward to hearing from you soon.

Sincerely,

Heather Moreno

August 9, 1999

Manchester Café
438 Third Street
Manchester, NH 03036

To Whom It May Concern:

I am writing in response to the Manchester Café's advertisement in the *New Hampshire Sunday News*. The position of part-time cashier greatly interests me as I have had similar jobs and greatly enjoyed them.

In September, I will be a full-time student at Notre Dame College. I am seeking a position such as yours that will permit me to attend classes and partly finance my education.

The enclosed resume illustrates my past experience working as a cashier at two retail food establishments. I would be pleased if you contacted me for an interview at your earliest convenience. Thank you.

Sincerely,

Elly G. Minch
245 Chaparral Drive
Chester, NH 03036
(603) 555-1364

Enclosure

July 1, 2000

Ronald Wright
Travel Tours
354 High St.
Springfield, OH 45501

Dear Mr. Wright:

Please accept this letter as my application for the travel agent position available at your firm.

I have just received my diploma from Yellow Springs High School and am eager to begin my career in the travel industry. Presently, I am enrolled in a Regional Occupational Program travel course and a computer course on the Apollo series. Furthermore, my present employment has enabled me to become an excellent word processor and given me experience in handling correspondence.

I feel that my educational and professional background represent the qualifications you desire for this position. I look forward to setting a date for an interview during which we can discuss the position and share our expectations.

Thank you in advance for your consideration.

Sincerely,

Tracey Warrick
467 Altivo Drive
Yellow Springs, OH 45387
(513) 555-1875
twarrick@aol.com

Marvin Hopkins
341 Beach Pines Drive
Olympia, WA 98505
July 28, 2000

Charlene Butterfield
Human Resources Office
Computech
11156 Broadway
Redmond, WA 98052

Dear Ms. Butterfield:

I have been extremely impressed by your firm's successful entrance into the highly competitive personal computer marketplace. The young and aggressive nature of Computech appeals to me.

As a recent graduate of Eastern Washington University in computer and information sciences, I am looking for a permanent position as a project engineer. Ideally, my employment would offer the possibility for advancement to a management position in research and development.

I worked with Microsoft during my summer vacations in 1998 and 1999. During my employment, I was a member of a four-person team that installed and implemented a 60-node 3Com 3Plus local area network. I have also provided both hardware and software support for Windows-compatible personal computers.

A resume is enclosed that reflects my academic, technical, and professional history. I am confident that my background in the computer industry would make me an asset to Computech.

I look forward to hearing from you soon. Thank you for your consideration.

Sincerely,

Marvin Hopkins
(206) 555-2397
marvinhop@msn.com

Douglas P. Shaw
191 Cuesta Way
Boise, ID 83706
(208) 555-8599

April 6, 2000

Eleanor Johnson
The Idaho Statesman
440 Lincoln St.
Boise, ID 83706

Dear Ms. Johnson:

I am writing to you with the hope that there is an opening for a photographer at your newspaper.

For four years, I have been a photographic assistant at Precious Moments Photography. I set up the lights and cameras, mix chemicals, develop film, and print photographs. As head photographer for my high school's yearbook, I took photographs of my classmates at sporting and social activities throughout the year. I have enclosed some of these photographs that were used in your newspaper's sports section.

I am hardworking, creative, and imaginative. I enjoy challenging work and perform well under pressure. I believe that these traits could be useful in highlighting news events for your newspaper.

I would appreciate the opportunity to meet with you to discuss any openings for photographers. I thank you for your consideration and look forward to hearing from you.

Sincerely,

Douglas P. Shaw

enclosures

MELISSA L. JUNG

1530 Hansen Lane
Dover, DE 19901
(302) 555-9401

June 12, 2002

Mr. John Schwartz
Dover Unified School District
287 Central Avenue
Dover, DE 19901

Dear Mr. Schwartz:

I am writing to inquire whether the Dover Unified School District has an opening for an elementary school teacher. Having a master's degree in education and experience as an assistant art teacher in your district, I feel that I am well-qualified to be a teacher.

My personal experience as a mother of four children and as a hostess for six foreign exchange students has taught me how to relate effectively with young people. In addition, I have demonstrated my firm commitment to the community by leading the fund-raising efforts for the new elementary school and serving meals to homeless people at the soup kitchen.

I would appreciate the opportunity to discuss my qualifications and abilities with you at length in an interview.

Sincerely,

Melissa L. Jung

765 Murphy's Lane
Arlington, VA 22207
(703) 555-3099

May 15, 2002

Mr. Paul Evans, Manager
Arlington Motors Service Department
4900 Speedway
Arlington, VA 22207

Dear Mr. Evans:

I am interested in becoming an automotive mechanic for Arlington Motors. I also would like to participate in the automotive training program that your dealership sponsors.

While attending Arlington High School, I took all the automotive courses offered as well as business math. During the past year, I have been a station attendant at the Arlington Shell where I have made minor repairs to customers' cars and helped the station's mechanics with major repairs. In my free time, I customize vans.

I would like to meet with you to discuss opportunities at Arlington Motors. I can be reached by telephone at (703) 555-3099. Thank you for your time.

Sincerely,

Roger Newton

BRIAN KANEKO
P.O. Box 4855
Stanford, CA 94309
(650) 555-1007

February 10, 2000

Ms. Judy Andrews
Mesa Engineering
3500 Camelback Drive
Phoenix, AZ 85032

Dear Ms. Andrews:

I would like to obtain an appointment with a representative of your firm to interview for the entry-level construction management position advertised at the Placement Center.

My education and work experiences have prepared me to contribute to Mesa Engineering. I will receive my master's degree in civil engineering from Stanford University in May. My course work has focused on construction management. In addition, my summer work experiences on projects have honed my technical and organizational skills.

A copy of my resume is enclosed for your evaluation. If you need further information, I will be pleased to provide you with the necessary materials.

I look forward to meeting with a representative of your firm to discuss my qualifications.

Sincerely,

Brian Kaneko

Enclosure

September 1, 2000

Dr. Diane Wilson
ACME Physical Therapy and Sports Rehabilitation Clinic
489 South First Avenue
Grand Rapids, MI 49505

Dear Dr. Wilson:

I am writing concerning possible employment opportunities with your clinic. In partic-ular, I am looking for an assistant physical therapist position that would permit me to work with physically disabled individuals while I attend college.

In September, I will start studies at Calvin College where I plan to major in education of the physically handicapped. I would be available for part-time work at that time.

I have had direct experience in dealing with physically disabled people. At Bay de Noc Camp, I was camp counselor for developmentally disabled teenagers and adults, and at Escanaba High School, I assisted the Special Education teacher.

I would be delighted to meet with you at your convenience to discuss opportunities at your clinic.

Sincerely,

Christianna M. Nelson
900 Bear Valley Drive
Escanaba, MI 49829
(906) 555-2380

275 Huntington Drive
Middlebury, VT 05753

August 9, 2000

Manager
Covington Inn
300 Main Street
Montpelier, VT 05602

Dear Manager:

I am writing in response to your advertisement in the August 8, 2000, issue of the *Times Argus*. I would appreciate the opportunity to talk to you about your inn's need for a preparation cook.

In Middlebury, I was the preparation cook for Denny's Restaurant. I was responsible for making all salads including Chef's, Caesar, and Shrimp Louis. This fall I will be attending the New England Culinary Institute in your city where I plan to major in food production, management, and services. I am confident that my past experience and present training would be of benefit to your inn's restaurant.

I have enclosed my resume for your consideration. I hope to have a chance to speak with you about the position.

Yours truly,

Dale Crivello
(802) 555-4294

enclosure

ELIZABETH M. LEIGH-WOOD

387 Sunny Hills Drive
Madison, WI 53711
(608) 555-1524

April 24, 2000

Ms. Lorraine Sorenson
Madison Community Recreation Center
1500 Third Avenue, SE
Madison, WI 53711

Dear Ms. Sorenson:

I am writing to follow up on our April 23rd telephone conversation about the lifeguard position. As we discussed, I have been certified in Standard First Aid and CPR. Furthermore, I was a lifeguard for Sunny Hills Neighborhood Club pool during the summer of 1998. In August, I will attend Cardinal Stritch University on a track scholarship.

If I meet your requirements, I would be available for employment from June 1st to August 15th when I start school.

My resume is enclosed as you requested. I look forward to hearing from you soon.

Sincerely,

Elizabeth M. Leigh-Wood

enclosure

217 Arthur Avenue
Omaha, NE 68103
(402) 555-5003

July 30, 2000

Bob Perkins, Superintendent
Sunburst Golf Course
One Sunburst Way
Lincoln, NE 85021

Dear Mr. Perkins:

I wish to apply for the position of assistant greenkeeper. John Niles of Oak Brook Golf Course told me about this opening and suggested that I contact you.

Currently, I am a nursery assistant at Sugar Hill Nursery in Omaha. In this position, I have become familiar with the care of many varieties of grasses, trees, plants, and shrubs. Also, I took horticulture and biology courses in high school. I am self-motivated and work well independently.

I will call you next week to follow up on this letter. Thank you in advance for your consideration.

Sincerely,

John Nowark

CRAIG L. HJORRING

31 Anderson Road • Fort Collins, CO 80523 • (303) 555-0469

February 10, 2001

Mr. Michael Chambers
Sports First
1874 Mountain Boulevard
Denver, CO 80203

Dear Mr. Chambers:

I would be very interested in talking with you about a marketing career at Sports First.

Presently, I am pursuing a bachelor's degree in business administration and management with an emphasis in marketing. I plan to graduate in May 2001.

During the past three summers, I have worked at Sutherland Sports Wear. I started as a sales representative and was promoted to assistant regional sales manager. The following are a few of my accomplishments that may interest your organization:

• Decreased advertising costs to 2.4 percent of sales.
• Increased sales by more than 20 percent each summer.
• Made industry contacts for joint venture opportunities.

I feel that my qualifications would enable me to be a productive member of your marketing team.

Enclosed is my resume for your review. I look forward to meeting with you to discuss employment opportunities at Sports First.

Sincerely,

Craig L. Hjorring

Enclosure

3089 McGlenn Drive
Jonesboro, AR 72402
(501) 555-9268
July 8, 2002

Dr. Melinda Cross
Cross Veterinary Hospital
378 Graham Road
Little Rock, AR 72202

Dear Dr. Cross:

I am interested in applying for employment as a manager at your veterinary hospital.

Recently, I graduated from Arkansas State University with a degree in biology. Also, I have six months of experience working as a veterinarian assistant. My duties included the administration of medicine and pacification of animals. I believe that my education and work experience would enable me to be a valuable asset to your hospital.

I would like to meet with you and demonstrate that I have the qualifications and the personality needed to make a successful hospital manager. I can be contacted at the above telephone number. Many thanks for your consideration.

Sincerely,

Nicole Anne Chang

Josephine Elizabeth Crocker

March 22, 2001

Ms. Louisa Brown, Director
Human Resources
New Jersey Health Department
P.O. Box 3000
Trenton, NJ 08625

Dear Ms. Brown:

This letter is in response to your advertisement for an environmental health inspector that appeared in the *Trentonian* on March 19, 2001. Please accept my resume in consideration for this position.

With a degree from Trenton State College in environmental health science and two internships with county health departments in the environmental division, I believe that I am well-suited to the state's health department needs.

Thank you for your time. I look forward to hearing from you soon regarding this position.

Sincerely,

Josephine E. Crocker
P.O. Box 317 A
Trenton, NJ 08625
(609) 555-4832

502 Sleigh Street
Stockton, CA 95211

January 11, 2000

Mr. Oliver Ford, Vice President
International Bank of New York
500 Broad Street
New York, NY 10050

Dear Mr. Ford:

I am writing to obtain further information regarding employment with your organization as a financial analyst. I strongly believe that international banking is an area in which my academic training, skill with languages and computers, and personal qualities would be an asset.

At the University of the Pacific, I am majoring in political science while also pursuing a business focus. Course work in accounting, statistics, and management has allowed me to develop the skills that are necessary to successfully perform financial analyses. Moreover, my past work experiences have provided me with opportunities to use and refine those skills in a business setting.

I appreciate your time and consideration. I hope to have the opportunity to talk with you in the near future.

Sincerely,

George Cox

Matt M. LeRoy

33 Pleasant Drive
Storm Lake, IA 50588
(712) 555-9232

September 28, 2002

Ms. Shari Fuller
Chicago Consultants Group
682 Market Street, Suite 10
Chicago, IL 60677

Dear Ms. Fuller:

I would greatly appreciate the opportunity to talk to you about your firm's need for a consultant analyst. I believe that my education at Iowa State University of Science and Technology in applied computer science and business administration as well as my work at Caterpillar, Inc., would be useful to your computer consulting group.

Working at Chicago Consultants Group would be a unique and challenging experience. Your company has attracted me by its size and reputation in the field of consulting.

Enclosed is my resume. Thank you for your consideration.

Sincerely,

Matt M. LeRoy
enclosure